ALL ABOUT

HERBS

First published in 1977 by
The Hamlyn Publishing Group Limited
London · New York · Sydney · Toronto
Astronaut House, Feltham, Middlesex, England
© Copyright The Hamlyn Publishing Group Limited 1977

Filmset by Tradespools Limited, Frome, Somerset, England
Printed by Hazell, Watson & Viney Limited,
Aylesbury, Buckinghamshire, England

ISBN 0 600 34531 9

ALL ABOUT
HERBS

Janet Dampney
and
Elizabeth Pomeroy

HAMLYN
London·New York·Sydney·Toronto

Acknowledgements

The publishers would like to thank the following for the illustrations used in this book: Photographie Giraudon (Paris), Iris Hardwick Library, Janet Dampney, Pat Brindley, Michael Warren, The Hamlyn Group Picture Library (London), The Mansell Collection (London), John Lee and International Magazine Service.

Line illustrations by **Marilyn Day**

Bibliography-Chapters I to VI

BROWNLOW, Margaret E.	Herbs and the Fragrant Garden	1957
CECIL, The Hon. Lady E.	A History of Gardening in England	1896
COATES, Alice M.	Flowers and their Histories	1956
CULPEPER, Nicholas	The English Physician	1652
GERARD, John	Herball	1597
HADFIELD, Miles	A History of British Gardening	1969
HERITEAU, Jacqueline	Potpourris and other Fragrant Delights	1975
HYLL, Thomas	The Gardener's Labyrinth	1577
LAWSON, William	The Country Housewife's Garden	1617
LOEWENFELD, Claire	Herb Gardening	1964
PAGE, M. and STEARN, William T.	Culinary Herbs (R. H. S. Wisley Handbook)	1974
PARKINSON, John	Paradisi in Sole Paradisus Terrestris	1629
ROHDE, Eleanor Sinclair	Herbs and Herb Gardening	1939
	The Old English Herbals	1922
SANECKI, Kay N.	The Complete Book of Herbs	1974
TUSSER, Thomas	Five Hundred Points of Good Husbandry	1573
WILSON, C. Anne	Food & Drink in Britain	1973

Contents

Useful Facts and Figures

Notes on metrication

In the recipes in this book quantities are given in metric, Imperial and American units of measure. As exact conversion from Imperial to metric does not always give very convenient working quantities it is standard practice to round off into units of 25 grams. The table below shows the recommended equivalents.

Ounces	Approx. g to nearest whole figure	Recommended conversion to nearest unit of 25
1	28	25
2	57	50
3	85	75
4	113	100
5	142	150
6	170	175
7	198	200
8	227	225
9	255	250
10	283	275
11	312	300
12	340	350
13	368	375
14	397	400
15	425	425
16 (1 lb)	454	450
17	482	475
18	510	500
19	539	550
20	567	575

Note When converting quantities over 20oz first add the appropriate figures in the centre column, then adjust to the nearest unit of 25. As a general guide, 1kg (1000g) equals 2.2lb or about 2lb 3oz. This method of conversion gives good results in nearly all cases but in certain cake recipes a more accurate conversion is necessary to produce a balanced recipe. On the other hand, quantities of such ingredients as vegetables, fruit, meat and fish which are not critical are rounded off to the nearest quarter of a kg as this is how they are likely to be purchased.

Liquid measures The millilitre has been used in this book and the following table gives a few examples:

Imperial	Approx. ml to nearest whole figure	Recommended ml
$\frac{1}{4}$ pint	142	150ml
$\frac{1}{2}$ pint	283	300ml
$\frac{3}{4}$ pint	425	450ml
1 pint	567	600ml
1$\frac{1}{2}$ pints	851	900ml
1$\frac{3}{4}$ pints	992	1000ml (1 litre)

Note For quantities of 1$\frac{3}{4}$ pints and over we have used litres and fractions of a litre.

Spoon measures All spoon measures given in this book are level.

Can sizes At present, cans are marked with the exact (usually to the nearest whole number) metric equivalent of the Imperial weight of the contents, so we have followed this practice when giving can sizes.

Linear measures Throughout the book linear measures have been given in metric units, followed by the Imperial equivalents in brackets. The following equivalents give a guide to the conversions used.

1cm = $\frac{1}{2}$ inch

2.5cm = 1 inch

30cm = 1 foot

1m = 3 feet

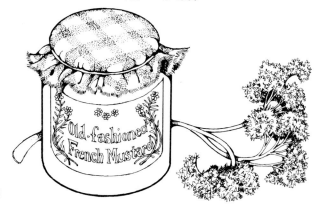

Oven temperatures
The table below gives recommended equivalents.

	°C	°F	Gas Mark
Very cool	110	225	$\frac{1}{4}$
	120	250	$\frac{1}{2}$
Cool	140	275	1
	150	300	2
Moderate	160	325	3
	180	350	4
Moderately hot	190	375	5
	200	400	6
Hot	220	425	7
	230	450	8
Very hot	240	475	9

Note When making any of the recipes in this book, only follow one set of measures as they are not interchangeable.

Notes for American users
Although the recipes in this book give American measures, the lists below give some equivalents or substitutes for terms and commodities which may be unfamiliar to American readers.

Equipment and terms
BRITISH/AMERICAN
cling film/saran wrap
cocktail stick/toothpick
frying pan/skillet
greaseproof paper/parchment paper
grill/broil
kitchen paper/paper towels
liquidize(r)/blend(er)
mince/grind
packet/package
polythene/plastic
roasting tin/roasting pan
stoned/pitted

Ingredients
BRITISH/AMERICAN
aubergine/eggplant
black olives/ripe olives
castor or granulated sugar/sugar
celery stick/celery stalk
chicory/Belgian endive
cooking apple/baking apple
cornflour/cornstarch
courgette/zucchini
desiccated coconut/shredded coconut
double cream/heavy cream
escalopes/scallops
essence/extract
French beans/green beans
glacé cherry/candied cherry
ham/cured or smoked ham
hard-boiled egg/hard-cooked egg
haricot beans/navy beans
icing sugar/confectioners' sugar
lard/shortening
natural yogurt/unflavored yogurt
plain flour/all-purpose flour
self-raising flour/self-rising flour, or all-
   purpose flour sifted with baking powder
single cream/light cream
spring onion/scallion
streaky bacon rasher/bacon slice
sultana/seedless white raisin
tomato purée/tomato paste
topside of beef/beef round
unsalted butter/sweet butter

Notes for Australian users
Ingredients in this book are given in cup, metric and Imperial measures. In Australia the American 8-oz measuring cup is used in conjunction with the Imperial pint of 20 fluid ounces. It is most important to remember that the Australian tablespoon differs from both the British and American tablespoons; the table below gives a comparison between the standard tablespoons used in the three countries. The British standard tablespoon holds 17·7 millilitres, the American 14·2 millilitres, and the Australian 20 millilitres. A teaspoon holds approximately 5 millilitres in all three countries.

British	American	Australian
1 teaspoon	1 teaspoon	1 teaspoon
1 tablespoon	1 tablespoon	1 tablespoon
2 tablespoons	3 tablespoons	2 tablespoons
$3\frac{1}{2}$ tablespoons	4 tablespoons	3 tablespoons
4 tablespoons	5 tablespoons	$3\frac{1}{2}$ tablespoons

Note The British and Australian pint is 20 fluid ounces as opposed to the American pint which is 16 fluid ounces.

Introduction

The increasing interest in growing and using herbs is very much a sign of the times. We are reacting strongly against the growing pollution of our natural heritage and the rising tide of synthetic laboratory products which flood the market.

While admitting the many advantages of modern science, particularly in medicine, and the convenience of the supermarkets with their pre-packed goods, we are re-awakening to the pleasure of home growing and home cooking, in which herbs and herb lore emerge as a fascinating and intrinsic part. Man through the centuries has used herbs in many ways, some of them devious, and much has been written about them. The more you experiment with herbs, the more intriguing they become.

Our major problem in writing this book has been in selecting which herbs to include from so wide and rich a field. Indeed we feel in sympathy with William Lawson, who wrote in 1631 in 'The Country Housewife's Garden': '. . . and though I knowe some have written well and truely and others more plentifully upon this theame, yet somewhat have I learned by experience . . . which hitherto I cannot find put into writing.'

Finally, we have chosen the herbs which we hope you will be able to grow yourself; fragrant, aromatic or pretty, sometimes all three, so you may decorate your garden, perfume your home or your person, and add fresh and subtle flavours to your cooking.

Janet Dampney.

Elisabeth Pomeroy

I
The History of Herbs

As we shine a torch backwards into history, the objects or facts close at hand are clear and unquestionable but into the distance we are left in the main to conjecture and even professional historians differ as to what they see. The swirling mists of legend, mythology and superstition make the early history of herbs tantalizingly difficult to trace but consequently all the more fascinating.

From his first appearance on the earth, man and his ape-like forebears have been dependent on plants both for their own sustenance and as food for the animals they hunted and eventually tamed and domesticated. The first plants used would be those they found as wild plants, but these soon spread to countries far from their native origin, taken by wandering tribes, and coriander came to Britain from the Mediterranean area as far back as the late Bronze Age.

When the Romans came to Britain in AD 43 they brought with them an inheritance of civilizations far older than our own, going back to ancient Greece, Babylon and Egypt. They used many herbs for cooking in recipes from ancient Greece. They grew many medicinal herbs guided largely by the writings of Pliny and the Greek, Dioscorides. They valued lavender and roses, especially for toilet waters and perfumes, and other herbs and flowers for the making of sweet-scented garlands and wreaths. Many herbs were no doubt introduced to Britain during this time but were lost again after the Romans departed in 430 AD.

The Saxons who took over some 70 years later were a primitive people and knowledge of the sophisticated use of herbs gradually disappeared during the Dark Ages.

Herbs in Magic and Medicine

The early Saxons had other reasons for growing and gathering herbs from the wild. Surrounded by eerie forests, wild heaths and moors, they attributed their sufferings, and particularly diseases, to evil spirits. The earliest existing Saxon book on herbs being used as medicinal plants is the Leech Book of Bald of about 900–950 AD which refers at considerable length to protection from 'elf-disease'. The people relied still on the old superstitions and heathen rites which went back beyond the worship of Woden and the religious rites of the Druids, to nature worship itself.

Herbs were gathered with great ceremony, usually at night, by people in white attire, and were then prepared with incantations. They were not only eaten but worn on the body as cures, and the sick-rooms were fumigated by surrounding hot stones with herbs on which cold water was poured — a similar practice to the use of incense in religious rites. Herbs were also elaborately prepared — not given to the sick person but thrown into running water to carry off the evil. The Church strictly forbade the use of incantations when gathering or preparing herbs and masses were sung in their place. Heathen myths were Christianized, but for centuries belief remained in the evil or the good influence of plants.

Angelica was believed to have special power against evil and was said to be named because a monk dreamt of an angel telling him of its power to cure the plague. The holy thistle (*Carduus benedictus*) was also used against the plague and was expected to cure all ills. The elder was held in special reverence as a symbol of love and protection but was also thought to be inhabited by a witch whose permission must be asked before it was cut. The periwinkle was also thought to have mysterious powers and was called the sorcerer's violet, being potent against the powers of evil and used in making love potions. The house leek (a valuable medicinal herb) was grown on roofs as a protection against lightning and bad luck. Rue was believed to enable one to see witches and take avoiding action! A mixture of rue and vervain was said to be used in the cauldron against evil spirits and to give magical powers to man. It became known as the 'herb of grace', no doubt because it was used to sprinkle holy water. Myth and magic of an evil kind surrounded the mandrake, the roots were thought to be in the shape of a man or woman and to grow wild only under gallows. When digging up the roots they were said to shriek and a dog was tied to the root so that the man should not be affected by the evil and die. But the mandrake roots boiled in wine promoted sleep and eased pain. Medicine gradually took over from the unseen and unknown powers of good and evil. But the witch in human form made full use of the potency of herbs and used them as her stock-in-trade for many centuries. Poisonous herbs such as hemlock were useful to kill off one's enemies or wild animals. The monkshood (aconitum) was called wolfsbane and used to poison bait for wolves, a particular menace to the people of medieval Britain.

As monasteries were established, particularly after the Norman Conquest, the monks, able to read the ancient Latin writings on herbs, obtained plants from their brother Orders on the Continent. Some came already dried and the word drug is derived from the Anglo-Saxon *drigan*, meaning 'to dry.' With a vocation to serve the poor and the sick, the monks grew many medicinal herbs in their

In the Middle Ages, the apothecary's shop carried a large stock of herbal remedies which were offered as cures for a multitude of ailments

gardens and acted as physicians to the surrounding neighbourhood until the dissolution of the monasteries in the time of Henry VIII. Herbs were used as remedies for all illnesses and accidents such as poisoning by the biting of snakes or mad dogs.

In the Middle Ages, as land gradually came into ownership other than the feudal lord, herbs were grown in the manor house gardens where the lady of the house would treat the minor ailments of her family, servants and surrounding neighbours, especially if they lived far from a monastery. She had her stillroom for the drying, preparing and distilling of herbs for medicinal and every other use. Only the rich could afford to call in a physician, but the apothecary had his shop for the sale of herbal remedies and this explains the second Latin name of so many herbs *officinalis* meaning 'of the shop'. Gradually the least educated must have learned to use the right herbs for minor ailments, to aid digestion, sleep and even one's memory! Depression, or 'melancholie' as it was then called, seems as now to have been a common affliction. Borage flowers in salad were said to 'exhilarate and make the mind glad' and they were often used with wine for the same purpose (as we use them still today). Lemon balm was also said to drive away 'heavyness of mind' and sweet woodruff to 'make the heart merry and help the liver'.

The Doctrine of Signatures was popular in the 16th and 17th centuries, many herbalists believing that God had imprinted on the plants a guide to their medicinal use. Plants with red juice or sap, such as St John's wort, were used for cuts and wounds; a yellow sap suggested jaundice, a walnut diseases of the brain, and the spotted leaves of lungwort (pulmonaria) a diseased lung (it was in fact used for tuberculosis until comparatively recently). Less

This 16th century woodcut shows a gardener tending his raised beds of herbs. Apart from displaying the plants well, such beds give the good drainage facilities which many herbs appreciate

As well as being cultivated for their curative properties many herbs were grown for the benefit of bees. In the 16th century sugar in Britain was scarce and expensive and honey was still the main sweetener of the day

widely held was the belief in astrology and the influence of the stars which was the faith of the famous Nicholas Culpeper and expounded in his herbal.

Herbals were first written for the guidance of physicians and apothecaries, but Gerard's great herbal of 1597 reached a far greater number and would be consulted for its minute description of each herb, where it could be found growing wild and all its 'virtues'. It repays reading again today both for the beauty of its language and the fascinating light it throws on, what is to us, strange plant lore of the time. Although much of this information is still accepted today he does occasionally stretch the imagination. For instance he tells us that geese grow from barnacles on logs in the sea — 'that which I have seen with mine eyes'. Gerard no doubt studied medicine as he had been apprenticed as a barber-surgeon but he was also a gardener and supervised the gardens of Lord Burleigh at Theobalds in Hertfordshire and in the Strand, and had a great collection of plants in his own garden at Holborn.

Medicine and botany were strongly linked and the first botanic gardens were attached to universities for the study of medicine. Our first botanic garden, constructed at Oxford in 1632, was first called a physic garden, and the Chelsea Physic Garden, started by the Society of Apothecaries in 1673, still retains this name.

Another famous writer on herbs was John Parkinson, apprenticed as an apothecary. His great work, Paradisi in Sole Paradisus Terrestris (1629) (a Latin pun on his name — Park-in-sun), was really more a gardening book than a herbal. It describes many plants other than those grown for culinary, medicinal and other uses (which we still today call herbs). The enjoyment of flowers and plants in a pleasure garden, for their beauty alone, was gradually taking precedence and orthodox medicine became less and less dependent on herbs.

Herbs in Early Gardens

The elaborate formal gardens made by the Romans disappeared during the Dark Ages along with many of the plants they had introduced. We can get the best idea of the earliest medieval gardens from illustrated manuscripts of the time, particularly the missals painted by the monks. Unfortunately almost all are from the continent, no doubt owing to the destruction of religious books at the reformation. The pattern of beds in a monastery garden was a series of rectangles with paths between to allow easy access to each bed. The physic garden would be separate and near the infirmary.

The checkerboard pattern was the favourite plan for the growing of herbs in medieval times and was used in the first botanic gardens. There are also manuscript paintings of gardens within castle walls, and tapestries in which we see features such as the 'flowery mead', with flowers growing in the turf — primroses, violets and daisies which could be cut for eating and used medicinally. Chaucer wrote 'full gay was all the ground'. Herbs were often grown in a bank of earth against a wall, supported by a base of stones or bricks, and there would be recesses for seats which would be of turf, and later chamomile was used. Much space would be given to vegetables and pot herbs.

It was important to have a beehive, honey being the main source of sweetening before sugar was imported. Many herbs were grown for the benefit of the bees and lemon balm was especially favoured as bees were thought never to leave a garden in which it was grown. Other herbs were grown for the strong scent of their flowers or leaves and were used for strewing the floors. One of the earliest gardening books by Thomas Tusser, dated 1573, lists twenty herbs for strewing including lavender, fennel, costmary, chamomile and the flowers of cowslips, daisies and roses. Furniture and floors were also scented and polished by pounding the seeds of sweet Cicely in a mortar and rubbing the juice over their surfaces.

Herbs were also grown for scents and toilet waters and for cosmetics to give the lady 'a fayre face'. Pomanders, holding a sponge or some moss, filled with scented waters were carried especially by priests and doctors visiting the sick. The dried orange stuck with cloves dates back to the time of Cardinal Wolsey. Saffron, woad, alkanet (a kind of anchusa) and other herbs were used as dye plants and soapwort was grown both medicinally and as a substitute for soap.

Although the gardens were filled with plants and flowers intended for some practical use, the garden was still enjoyed as a place of rest, quiet and privacy. To this end there were arbours covered with sweet-scented honeysuckle or roses such as sweetbriar, and sometimes juniper. Lawns and garden walks were planted with chamomile, thyme and salad burnet. In church and monastery gardens flowers would be grown, particularly lilies, roses and peonies, for decorating the altar and for festivals and ceremonial occasions, and the Tudor garden had flowers and sweet smelling herbs to cut for nosegays. Rosemary was a favourite wall shrub of the Elizabethans and earlier Sir Thomas More wrote, 'I lette it runne all over my garden walls not only because my bees love it but because it is a herb sacred to remembrance and therefore to friendship'.

Rosemary was sometimes grown at the centre of a maze planted with low-growing ever-

green herbs and was also often used as a hedge to surround the elaborate knot garden which was, in the early 16th century, becoming fashionable. A formal pattern was outlined with herbs such as cotton lavender, thyme, marjoram, hyssop or germander. An 'open knot' was filled with flowers. A 'closed knot' was a more complicated pattern with no flowers but sands or brick dust might be used to give contrasting colours. By the time Parkinson was writing on the knot garden in 1629, box, with no herbal value, was the favourite plant to form the knot pattern and the open knots were filled with flowers 'all planted in some proportion one unto another as is fit for them which will give such grace to the garden that will seem like a piece of tapestry of many glorious colours'. The herb was no longer the centre of the garden stage and has never returned!

This revolution in gardening was partly due to many new plants coming from abroad. The Tradescants, father and son, were particularly zealous in their search for new plants and many came through them from Virginia and other parts of the New World. It was, however, a two-way traffic; the Pilgrim Fathers took many herbs with them and John Josselyn, who visited the country some time later, made a list of those which did well and those which died in the colder winters of New England — 'Southernwood is no plant for this Country, Nor Rosemary, Nor Bayes', he wrote.

Bergamot is probably the only herb we still grow in Britain today which came to us from the New World. *Monarda didyma*, the scarlet bergamot from Oswego on Lake Ontario, bloomed first in England in 1744 from seed raised by Peter Collinson. This was the plant which made the Oswego tea, famous from the time of the Boston Tea Party. It was used as a substitute for the East India Company's tea which was thrown into Boston harbour by the colonists and it is used to flavour the well known Earl Grey tea today.

The herb had no place in the 18th century landscape garden or the Victorian bedding schemes, but through the centuries it has been grown in the true cottage garden which is so fast disappearing as the cottager moves to the council estate.

Cooking with Herbs

The Romans brought with them to Britain an entirely new style of cooking. Elaborate sauces were prepared for both fish and meat, and new herbs, vegetables and fruits such as the vine were introduced. Some of the familiar herbs they brought with them were rosemary, sage, garden thyme, hyssop, savory, sweet marjoram, garlic, chervil, dill, coriander and fennel. The last two now grow wild in Britain and are thought to be escapes from cultivation.

Many of the Romans' recipes were strongly spiced and sausages and black pudding particularly were flavoured with pepper, cumin, rue, parsley and other herbs. All this culinary art was lost in the Dark Ages and herbs were not used extensively again in cookery until the early Middle Ages when they were reintroduced, largely through the influence of the Norman Conquest. The Monastery gardens, as well as the physic gardens already mentioned, had a large kitchen garden where many vegetables and herbs were grown and used by the monks, many of whom lived on a meatless diet.

English cooking was strongly influenced by the French cuisine of the Normans. For example, whereas sage was the accepted English flavouring for sausages, the Normans used fennel and powdered spices. The poor lived mainly on pottage, a vegetable or meat broth flavoured with herbs and thickened with corn, barley or oatmeal. This was enriched with butter, if it was available, and occasionally eggs. Parsley was a favourite medieval flavouring herb, both the leaves and roots being used. Fennel (both leaves and seeds), sage, thyme, mint and savory were also used and green pottages and sauces were made entirely of green vegetables and herbs. A green sauce for fish recommended in the 12th century includes sage, parsley, costmary, thyme and garlic. The strong flavour of the latter was especially valued and no doubt its antibiotic action on the intestines was particularly important in those times, though it was less favoured in the reign of Elizabeth I.

There were also flower pottages using primroses, violets and mallow, and elder flowers were used in a filling for tarts. Medieval salads were colourful mixtures of herbs and flowers, using such blooms as violets, primroses, mari-

golds, borage, and the clove carnation or 'gilloflower'. This practice continued into Tudor and Stuart times when the nasturtium came to us from the West Indies to add even more colour, as well as the hot flavour of its leaves.

Herbs were especially valued for stuffings, seasonings and sauces to disguise tainted meat. If fodder was lacking during the winter, animals were slaughtered in large numbers and the meat preserved in salt. The rich fed almost entirely on meat and game birds, as opposed to the largely vegetable pottages which supported the poor, particularly in medieval times. Meat pottage was a popular dish in Tudor and Stuart Britain and it was flavoured with onions or with the juice of herbs from the mortar. In Scotland, a dish called Skink was made with chopped leg of beef flavoured with saffron and herbs.

Saffron was grown commercially from early times, mainly in the eastern counties. It was used for colouring and flavouring and was always an expensive luxury — thousands of the stigmas of the crocus-like flowers being needed to produce a comparatively small amount of saffron.

From Elizabethan times rose petals and other flowers such as violets were candied as sweetmeats and for decoration. Cooking was much influenced by French recipes during the Stuart period, in the time of Mary Queen of Scots and after the restoration of Charles

II. It became fashionable to perfume food during the 16th and 17th centuries and roses were grown to make rosewater which was used both in cooking and medicinally. The 'faggot of sweet herbs' (which we now call bouquet garni) was also introduced at this time.

With the opening up of trade with the East, through the East India Company, many new spices arrived in Britain and began to replace the herb as popular flavourings. The quality of meat improved; the rich now had ice houses in which to store their meat, and sauces became simpler. Parsley or mint sauce, with one herb alone, replaced the complicated green sauces of medieval times, and towards the end of the 18th century came the first bottled sauces produced commercially.

During the 18th century, the grand tour of Europe undertaken by the rich and educated introduced them not only to continental art and architecture, but to its cooking, and chefs were brought over and employed in this country. However, the majority could neither grow nor afford the ingredients for this type of cooking. With the Industrial Revolution and 'back-to-back' housing in larger and larger towns, the former countryman with his vegetable plot and herbs in the cottage garden was replaced by the townsman relying largely on cheap starchy foods and puddings, frequently ready cooked.

Herbs Today

The knowledge of the medicinal uses of herbs has lingered on in country districts and many of the older generation now living in towns can remember the herbs which grew in the gardens of their childhood and how they were used. Although the medical profession has become less and less dependent on herbs, they are largely used in homoeopathy and by modern herbalists. The natural herb is less likely to produce side effects than the modern extraction and synthetic drugs, and there is a renewed interest in the use of herbs for minor ailments and for their health-giving properties. We are learning again to value the scents of pot-pourri and herbal sachets; the pleasure of using rosemary, for instance, as a hair rinse; the herbal preparations used as cosmetics, and above all herbs in cookery. Since the last war travel has been possible for many people, not only the rich. Young and old tour the continent and the younger generation particularly have returned inspired to more adventurous cooking, using and wishing to grow the herbs they have tasted in their travels.

And so our gardens are changing to grow these plants so long neglected and the herb is returning if not to the centre of the stage at least to a valued place among our shrubs, flowers and vegetables.

II
Herb Cultivation

Some of you will already be experienced gardeners, others will perhaps be cooks who have found that fresh herbs are expensive and not always easy to buy and that the choice is very limited. It is usually confined to mint and parsley, occasionally chives, sage and rosemary, and increasingly coriander leaves in districts with an immigrant population accustomed to the stronger flavours of Eastern cooking. The following information is then mainly given to help the new gardener and does not apply entirely to herb growing.

Growing Conditions

Success with plants depends on giving them the conditions they enjoy, similar, in fact, to those found where they grow wild. Some plants will grow almost anywhere and hence become weeds; we usually have no difficulty in growing these!

Soil
The soil is, of course, of great importance. In Britain we have a wide range of soils from heavy, sticky clays to light soils which are almost entirely composed of sand or even gravel and stones. Between these extremes are the loams, which may be heavy, with a large proportion of clay, or they may be lighter and more sandy. Lucky is the gardener who has a loam soil and the herb gardener who has a light loam, rather than a heavy one. There can, however, be problems with very sandy or stony soils because the drainage is so sharp that some plants will suffer in dry weather. Fortunately many of the herbs we grow come from Mediterranean countries and grow in just such soils on mountain sides. They are especially adapted to withstand these conditions and this was particularly noticeable during the devastating drought of the 1976 summer in Britain. These stony, sandy soils are called 'hungry' because they quickly lose plant foods as the water drains rapidly through.

Humus
Humus is obtained from rotting organic matter and if added to the soil will help most herbs to grow more strongly and produce more growth and leaves to cut. It acts like a sponge, holding moisture,

and greatly benefits herbs which resent drying out too much. Chervil, parsley, chives, mint, bergamot, angelica and lovage all like a moisture-retentive soil.

Farmyard manure provides rich humus which is not recommended for the majority of herbs, encouraging too much growth which lacks flavour and does not withstand the winter cold so well. There are exceptions, and mint responds particularly to well rotted manure dug in before planting.

Composting

Every gardener should have a compost heap where all suitable surplus green material from the garden and kitchen can be rotted down for eventual return to the soil. Comfrey leaves which have been allowed to wilt for twenty-four hours are an excellent activator. Instructions for making compost heaps are found in all good gardening books and, although space for stacking compost is difficult to find in tiny gardens, there are many types of bin now available which are neat and convenient to use. The humus from compost is ideal for herbs and that derived from leafmould is equally valuable.

Fallen leaves can be added to the compost heap but if you have any quantity it is best to rot them down separately. I find the most practical method is to fill large polythene bags with damp leaves. Avoid those from evergreens, chestnut (whose leaves have hard stems) and tough sycamore and plane leaves which rot down very slowly. Beech, oak, apple and garden shrubs such as forsythia are ideal. They will rot down more quickly if you pack them in firmly, sprinkling among them a compost activator or superphosphate of lime as you go. An 8-cm (3-in) flower pot of the powder should be enough for the average sized bag. Pierce a few holes in the side, bend over the top and weight it with a heavy stone or brick.

Store it outside or in a cool garden shed and by the following autumn you will have crumbly leafmould to use either in preparing a herb bed or for mulching existing plants, that is, laying it on the surface of the soil around them. This protects the roots in winter and worms will carry it down to enrich the soil.

Soil Improvement

Many people rely on peat to provide humus but it is expensive to use in large amounts. It provides little or no plant food but helps enormously to improve the texture of heavy soils and to hold moisture in the dry sandy ones. If bought in a dry state it must be soaked before use. I find it particularly useful for putting in the hole around the roots when planting in difficult soil, and especially for moisture-loving plants.

Gritty material such as coarse sand will improve heavy soils, and sieved coal ash (with the finer dust removed) is well worth using, though it should first be allowed to weather outdoors for three months to wash out the sulphur. In cases where soil is very waterlogged it may be necessary to lay a permanent underground drain system.

One of the chief problems with heavy soils is the difficulty in making a fine enough texture for seed sowing and the most difficult herbs to grow will be those which require sowing direct into the soil, resenting the disturbance to the roots which comes from sowing in boxes and planting out. Improving heavy soils is a slow process and it is best to concentrate on a small area at first and to choose those herbs which are most likely to flourish. Sage, fennel and thyme do surprisingly well, as do mint, chives and parsley, though it is not advisable to sow the latter directly into the ground.

Many herbs prefer an alkaline soil which, in Britain, is caused by the presence of chalk or limestone. Sometimes alkaline topsoil is heavy clay, cancelling out its particular value for herbs. But I am lucky to garden in North Oxfordshire where the soil is alkaline but a light loam, so I have ideal conditions for many herbs and particularly the decorative silver-leaved plants: lavender, santolina, southernwood, wormwood, sage and the curry plant.

It is well worth buying a simple soil testing kit to test for what is called the pH of a soil; that is, whether it is acid or alkaline. On the pH scale, 7 is neutral, numbers above this indicate an alkaline soil and those below, an acid soil. A very wide range of plants will grow in a neutral or slightly acid soil and even the more acid soils can easily be made suitable for lime-loving herbs by adding ground limestone or hydrated lime at the rates recommended on your testing kit instructions. Do be careful not to overlime or spread it around in parts of the garden where you may decide later that you wish to grow acid-loving plants such as azaleas and rhododendrons.

Sun and Shade

Plants growing in the wild are adapted to grow best in varying degrees of sun and shade. Many herbs native to the Mediterranean need sun to ripen the seeds, to harden growth so that it can withstand the winter, and also to produce the aromatic oils and flavouring and valuable vitamins and minerals for which we grow them. It may seem strange that the best oil of lavender can be grown in Britain, Mitcham lavender being the most famous. This is because in sunshine which is too hot much of the oil of lavender becomes volatile and is lost. Town gardeners with often high surrounding walls and sometimes large trees may have little space for sun-loving herbs and here built-up beds supported by a low wall will be a great advantage. The plants will be nearer the light, the drainage will be good and the

Old tapestries, like this one from Florence, give an insight into the layout of 16th century gardens

more prostrate herbs such as thyme and savory can be planted to fall down the sides. New gardens in the country with no established trees or shrubs will, of course, have little shade but herbs can be planted on the northern side of quick-growing taller annuals and perennials, where at least they will be shaded in the hotter summer months.

The less hardy plants such as rosemary and particularly lemon verbena must have not only hot sun but shelter from cold winds and, in most parts of the country, must have a south-facing wall behind them. Woodruff and angelica need no sun to grow well but a number of herbs enjoy half shade, that is, where they only get sun for part of the day or filtered sun from nearby trees. Mint, parsley, sorrel, chives, lovage, comfrey and chervil (in summer) are examples.

Where to Grow Your Herbs

By now I am sure you will agree that it is more important to plant herbs where they will grow best rather than in the most convenient spot near the kitchen door, though it is ideal of course if we can do both. Many herbs are most suitable for planting in rows in the kitchen garden, particularly where a number of plants are required of herbs such as chervil or sorrel, or those grown mainly for seed, such as caraway and coriander. Others, particularly decorative-leaved plants (and here I would include all varieties of sage and some varieties of mint), can be planted with good effect in mixed borders with other plants. Decorative herbs are described in more detail in Chapter III. Parsley and chives make pretty edging plants to paths; thymes can be planted in the rock garden and there are a number of creeping low-growing

herbs suitable for planting in paving or on a bank. This I consider the best approach for those with small or even average-sized gardens but I have to admit that if your garden is large enough, an area entirely devoted to herbs can be a haven of beauty, peace and old-world charm. I think particularly of the walled herb garden at Cranborne Manor in Dorset, a simple arrangement of squared beds surrounded and divided by grass paths. The beds are edged with low hedges of cotton lavender and a great variety of culinary and medicinal herbs have been planted with great artistry. The scent from this garden on a warm day after rain has been for me a quite unforgettable experience.

Herbs in Containers

A patio can be described as a paved area adjoining the house where most if not all the plants are grown in containers. The area is usually sheltered from cold winds and provided it is open to sunshine, or at least not heavily overhung with trees, a great variety of herbs can be grown. The choice will largely depend on whether you are mainly concerned to have an attractive place to sit and relax or whether it is to be primarily a collection of herbs for use in the kitchen. We will assume that you want both of these things and are prepared to make a reasonable compromise.

Any plant will grow in a container for a limited period provided that the soil is suitable and there is sufficient room for the roots. Some plants adapt better than others and many, in fact, benefit from this restriction. However, there must be room for the root system to obtain sufficient moisture and food to keep the plant growing healthily. Adequate drainage is essential and a hole or holes must be made in the base of the pot, tub or window box. Over the holes should be a layer of broken clay flower pot, small stones or

failing this broken pieces of polystyrene. It is best to cover these with a layer of peat or leafmould to prevent the compost gradually washing down and blocking the free drainage of water.

Compost Plants in containers need a richer soil than those growing in the garden and most people find it convenient to buy John Innes potting compost No. 2 which is a standard mixture of loam, peat and sand with a balanced fertilizer added. Unfortunately good loam is in short supply and the quality of compost suffers leading usually to compaction. This can be overcome by adding a little extra moist peat. The compost should always be moist when used and should not be kept for more than three months after mixing. In spite of the sometimes poor quality of John Innes compost, I prefer it to the peat-based loamless compost for outdoor containers. Less frequent feeding is necessary and the weight of the soil keeps the plant anchored more securely in the pot. It is cheaper to make up your own compost if you have your own good loam as a basis and mix in peat or leafmould and sand, for good drainage, and a fertilizer such as bonemeal, but the town gardener is well advised to buy a ready-mixed compost. Never fill containers entirely to the top, but allow room for watering; 1 to 5cm ($\frac{1}{2}$ to 2in) should be allowed according to the size of the pot, tub or box.

Choice of Container Herbs look well in simple containers of wood or pottery and there are specially shaped pots for herbs where plants can be grown from the sides as well as the top. These can look very attractive but they do dry out rather quickly and the large number of roots can exhaust the soil making extra feeding necessary. The inside of wooden tubs or boxes should be treated with a

A built-up bed in the corner of a patio, together with a few pots and containers, can provide an attractive display of useful culinary herbs.

1. Rosemary
2. Sweet marjoram
3. Nasturtium
4. Purple sage
5. Fennel
6. Sage
7. Parsley
8. Golden-varie-gated lemon thyme
9. Chives
10. Garden thyme
11. Golden marjoram
12. Lemon thyme
13. Fern-leaved parsley
14. Mint
15. Basil
16. Chervil
17. Sweet Cicely
18. Bay
19. Tarragon
20. Salad burnet

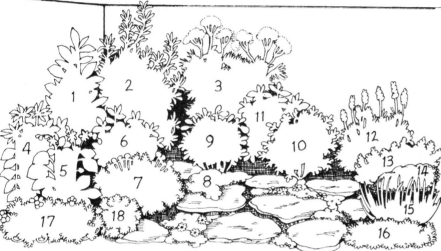

A sunny corner of the garden makes a good home for a mixture of culinary and decorative herbs. Creeping plants such as thyme, chamomile and pennyroyal will thrive in the crevices between paving stones, and stepping stones give easy access to plants at the back of the border.

1 Bay
2. Rosemary
3. Black fennel
4. Bergamot (pink)
5. Borage
6. Annual clary (pink)
7. Cotton lavender
8. Thyme (Silver Queen)
9. Purple-leaved sage
10. Rue (Jackman's Blue)
11. Perennial clary
12. Lavender
13. Hyssop
14. Golden thyme
15. Chives
16. Winter savory
17. Curry plant
18. Parsley

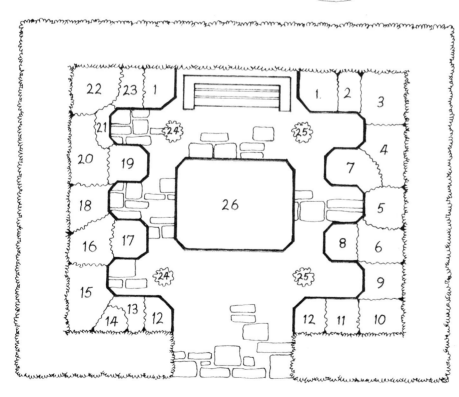

A formal herb garden surrounded by a yew hedge. The arrangement of the paving gives access to each herb.

1. Lavender
2. Damask rose
3. Angelica
4. Lemon balm
5. Lovage
6. Bergamot
7. Sage
8. Southernwood
9. Sweet Cicely
10. Tansy
11. Parsley
12. Winter savory
13. Chives
14. Borage
15. Rosemary
16. Fennel
17. Wormwood
18. Coriander
19. Tarragon
20. Lemon verbena
21. Basil
22. Bay
23. Gallica rose
24. Chamomile
25. Creeping thyme
26. Pink roses sur-rounded by thymes, marjorams and pinks

Thyme makes a superb edging plant, particularly when grown alongside a stone-flagged path

preservative such as cuprinol. I find that several plants together in a larger container such as a window box often do better than when they are each grown in separate pots. One thing is certain; that plants bought in garden centres in 8-cm (3-in) pots must quickly be potted on into something larger. I find the half-depth 13-cm (5-in) pots in which florists sell chrysanthemums and other flowering plants are ideal for most smaller-growing herbs such as thyme, parsley and marjorams, but I find that chives and mint do better in a larger pot as much as 18cm (7in) across. Mint will appreciate some well-rotted manure or compost in the bottom of the pot for extra nourishment, and being so invasive is best planted alone. Strong-growing plants such as fennel will eventually need a 25-cm (10-in) pot but you can keep the plants to about 45cm (18in) high by frequent cutting.

Aftercare Always remember that plants in containers dry out much more quickly than those in the open ground, and rain may be prevented from reaching the soil by overhanging leaves and branches. This is particularly liable to happen with bay trees, and the leaves will soon brown at the edges. Bay is, however, an ideal patio plant and shrubs such as rosemary, lavender, cotton lavender and the curry plant all do well.

An especially pretty plant for a pot is salad burnet and I also find the fern-leaved parsley more attractive and stronger growing than ordinary parsley, especially if the pot has to be left outside in winter.

One of the great assets of plants growing in pots is the ease with which they can be moved around into sun or shade as they seem to require it; also it is easier to protect them in winter if necessary. Heavy tubs can be put on to castors. If possible, find room for

a cold frame, here you can raise your own seedlings and cosset newly potted plants in a close atmosphere if necessary. You can strike cuttings at almost any time of the year according to the plant, and in winter it will give shelter for pot plants so that you can begin to cut from them much earlier in the spring. It is not only the patio gardener who will find a cold frame invaluable. It will benefit every gardener. Plants grown in pots will need feeding with a liquid fertilizer from time to time during the growing season, especially those such as mint, parsley, chives and chervil which benefit from richer soils. Each spring decide whether plants need larger pots or fresh soil. If the pot seems large enough and repotting unnecessary or impracticable, stale soil can be removed from the surface (taking care not to damage roots) and replaced with fresh soil.

Herbs on Balconies and Roofs
All that has so far been said on container gardening applies to balconies and roof gardens. But here there are special problems, the chief being exposure to wind, and some shelter from north-easterly wind must be provided especially for the more tender evergreens which will suffer during the winter. It depends how much trouble you are prepared to take — either grow plants which die down in winter or can be protected in a

cold frame, or plants which can be shrouded in polythene bags. Cotton lavender, though not a culinary herb, is exceptionally tough and will survive the cold winds of winter and the blazing heat of summer with equal enjoyment.

The heat reflected from the surface of a balcony or roof garden can be another problem and a surface of small stones which can be damped over during hot weather will be a great help to many plants. On the other hand, the extra sun and light which plants receive on balconies and roof gardens can give excellent results.

Herbs in Window Boxes
Given adequate drainage and a suitable compost, many herbs can be grown in one window box. The width should be at least 20cm (8in) and the depth 20 to 25cm (8 to 10in) to allow adequate root room for average-sized plants. The box is best raised from the level of the sill to assist drainage and prevent rotting of the base if it is made of wood.

Window boxes above ground level have the good light suggested as one of the assets for healthy growth on balconies and roof gardens. This means that even north-facing boxes will grow thyme, sages and savory and even basil if there is reasonable shelter from wind. Parsley, chives, dill, chervil and salad burnet should all do well. Sorrel will prefer an acid soil and mint will be best grown separately as already recommended. Some suggestions for including decorative herbs will be made in Chapter III.

A window box outside the kitchen window will be a special boon on those dark wet evenings when you have forgotten to bring in a supply from the garden! Herbs can also be planted in hanging baskets; especially suitable are parsley, thyme, winter or summer savory and sweet marjoram, with nasturtiums to add colour.

Growing Herbs Indoors

Indoor growing of herbs can be very disappointing especially when plants are started from seed. The seedlings can so quickly become weak and drawn and it is very difficult to get a mature healthy plant. One exception is parsley which must be resown two or three times a year as the older plants lose vigour. Much depends on the aspect of your window and a large bay window facing south will give the most scope.

On the whole I suggest that the indoor gardener buys culinary herbs as established plants, pots them on as necessary in the mixture suggested for container growing and feeds them regularly. They should be regarded as expendable.

Scented-leaved geraniums are an excellent choice and the lemon-scented variety is particularly easy to grow. It can be used for flavouring and dried for pot-pourri. Lemon verbena would be another good choice, but must be carefully pruned to prevent it from becoming straggly. Both these plants root easily from cuttings and the indoor gardener can raise other plants in this way especially with the help of a small propagator. This is much more rewarding than trying to raise plants from seed.

Although not strictly herbs, orange, lemon, tangerine and grapefruit pips germinate easily and make attractive pot plants. The lemons are especially attractive. Seeds should be soaked overnight and planted 1cm ($\frac{1}{2}$in) deep in a peaty compost. Put in a seed propagator or in a polythene bag in the airing cupboard, they will germinate in about a fortnight. The leaves can eventually be used for decoration or even flavouring, if you are not too attached to the plant to remove them!

Selecting Herbs for Your Garden

Choosing which herbs to grow will depend on your preferences and whether you can give them the conditions they require. Most cooks like to have fresh parsley, mint, chives, sage, rosemary, thyme and bay and may well be growing these successfully. Add to your collection each year by planting one or two of the less commonly grown kinds. Having made a list you must then decide whether to buy seeds or plants.

Length of Life

The A to Z will be a quick reference as to whether each plant is annual, biennial, perennial, shrub or tree.

Annuals complete their whole life cycle from seed in one season and then die. They are usually listed as hardy or half hardy, the latter term meaning that they can be killed off by frost if planted too soon.

Biennials do not reach maturity and flower until the year after the seed is sown and, again, they then die. If you are growing the plant for its leaves this is not important, in fact parsley leaves are at their best during the first year. On the other hand if you grow the plant for its flowers or seeds, for example caraway, patience is needed.

Perennials live on from year to year and the term is usually applied to herbaceous plants which die down more or less to the ground in winter, the other perennials are either shrubs or trees. These may be evergreen, or they may lose their leaves in winter, in which case they are called deciduous.

This will be elementary knowledge to many but is important to bear in mind when making your shopping list. Garden centres, nurseries and herb farms all have pot-grown plants for sale and because the labour cost is much the same, annuals will usually be as expensive as perennials so the latter will be much better value. Pot-grown hardy annuals are expensive to buy unless time for seed sowing is a very limiting factor. I would possibly make an exception for the half-hardy annuals which are more trouble to grow, and raising fifty spindly seedlings from a packet of seed is no comfort if you only want one good healthy plant.

Obtaining Plants

Buy or order your plants from a specialist herb nursery if possible; this will be essential if you want to grow any of the more unusual herbs. Most garden centres have a supply but the choice will be comparatively restricted. Decorative plants not usually listed as herbs, such as golden elder, bergamot and variegated thymes, are best obtained from specialist shrub, herbaceous or alpine nurseries as appropriate.

All the large seed firms have herbs on their lists but again a specialist nursery sometimes supplying both seeds and plants will have a larger choice.

Below: *Angelica* (Angelica archangelica)

Right: *Low-growing herbs like the ornamental sages and the golden-leaved marjoram look especially at home when mixed with taller plants such as foxgloves*

Good Garden Herbs

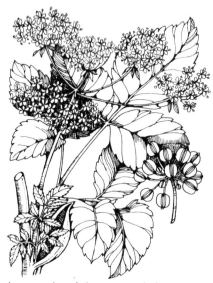

ANGELICA (*Angelica archangelica*)

The angelica grown for centuries in herb gardens is a native plant of northern Europe, even as far north as Lapland and Iceland, and has become naturalized in Britain. We have our own wild angelica but it is a different plant with a more bitter flavour. Great care in correct identification must of course be taken before using wild plants in the kitchen; some of them, such as hemlock, are extremely poisonous.

Once established, angelica is a large plant but it may be several years before it sends up its beautiful rounded heads of greenish-yellow flowers which gradually turn to brown as the seeds ripen. The flower stems in midsummer may be 2m (6ft) or more high and the large, bright green, cut and divided leaves may give the plant at least a metre spread. All parts of the plant produce a pleasant aromatic scent when bruised. It grows best in well-drained but moist soil in some shade. It is a short-lived perennial which dies after flowering and seeding, and you can prolong its life by not allowing it to do so.

Angelica is usually grown from seed but if you are impatient it is worth buying a container-grown plant which will mature much more quickly, having already had a start of probably six months. If you want a number of plants it is much cheaper to buy seed or ask a gardener friend to save some for you. It should be sown as soon as it is ripe in late summer; older seed usually fails to germinate. Sow it directly into the ground where you want the plants to grow, and then gradually thin them out using the removed seedlings for flavouring or for planting elsewhere in the garden. The space eventually taken up by each plant will vary according to the richness and dampness of your soil but expect to allow for 1m (3ft) or more between the plants when fully developed.

Large plants do not move easily but roots can be carefully divided and replanted preferably in the spring rather than in autumn. It is chiefly the leaf stems and leaves which are used for flavouring through the spring and summer, but do not cut them from a very young plant.

The flower stems are best for crystallizing and should be cut in late spring before they become too tough. Leaves for drying should also be cut in early summer and dried carefully in the dark as suggested for other herbs. They will have all the uses given in the A to Z section.

Angelica is a strikingly decorative plant in the garden and much appreciated by flower arrangers for its leaves, flowers and seed heads. It can be grown in a tub but really looks best in the border or wild garden.

ANISE (*Pimpinella anisum*)

Anise is seldom seen in gardens but its pretty clusters of tiny white flowers and its delicate feathery leaves make it a half-hardy annual well worth adding to your seed list, especially if you like the distinctive flavour of its leaves. You may also have a bonus of seeds to save if the summer is good.

Being a native of Greece, Crete, Asia Minor and Egypt it needs a well-drained soil and a sunny, sheltered position. Sow the seed in late spring where you want the plants to grow, remembering that they will grow to a height of about 45cm (18in). As the seedlings develop, thin them out leaving them finally about 23cm (9in) apart. Keep the plants well watered in dry weather.

Fresh leaves can be used all summer. If and when the heads are brown with seeds, cut them before they are ready to drop, and dry them.

BASIL (*Ocimum basilicum*)

Though a perennial plant in its native India and South-east Asia, basil must be treated in Britain as a half-hardy annual and grown free from frost. It makes a bushy plant usually about 45cm (18in) high and its glossy green leaves can be 5cm (2in) long if well grown. In late summer it will produce tiny white flowers but these are best pinched out to encourage more leafy growth.

Pot-grown plants are usually available from nurseries and garden centres in early summer but if you want several plants it is much cheaper to raise your own from seed. This will be easiest if you have a greenhouse or cold frame. As the seedlings resent disturbance sow a pinch to an 8-cm (3-in) pot — peat pots are ideal. Then thin out if necessary before

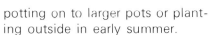

potting on to larger pots or planting outside in early summer.

Seed can also be sown outdoors in early summer where the plants are to grow. A warm sheltered spot with good, well-drained soil will give best results, especially if the plants are kept moist in dry spells. Pinching out the tips will keep the plants bushy, encourage new growth, and prevent flowering which exhausts them unnecessarily. Plants may be dug up in late summer, potted, trimmed back and brought into a frost-free greenhouse or sunny window for a supply of fresh leaves in winter.

Basil is difficult to dry successfully as the rather succulent leaves lose moisture slowly, and easily turn black or lack flavour. Cut the stems in late summer just before flowering and lay them on nylon netting in a dark, slightly warm airy place. Do not hang in bunches as this delays the drying process.

Basil can be grown very successfully in a pot or window box both in and out of doors in summer. As a pot plant I like to grow bush basil. This only grows about 30cm (1ft) high and has smaller leaves, slightly less aromatic but on a prettier and hardier plant.

BAY (*Laurus nobilis*)
Bay is the true laurel which the Romans used to crown their heroes and with which we honour our poet laureate. Its upward growing branches and dark green leaves give it an almost cypress-like spire which adds a pleasant, slightly Mediterranean atmosphere to our gardens, patios and front doors. Native in fact to the Mediterranean, it is not fully hardy in all parts of Britain, and needs to be planted in a sheltered position or at least moved to one in winter if it is in a tub. It can grow to 9m (30ft) or more, but by careful pruning it can be kept to a shrubby plant. It is often formally clipped to a pyramid or ball on a stem; particularly good shapes for tubs.

Spring planting is best and it prefers a sunny position but grows in any reasonably good soil. A mulch of manure (or hoof and horn meal and peat) in spring will help it to grow more vigorously, and plants in tubs will need a good compost.

It is very important not to spoil the shape of the tree when cutting bay leaves for the kitchen. If leaves are removed carefully little actual pruning is necessary, but should a tree be neglected you can prune out quite large sprays in late spring to improve the shape and make the plant more bushy. Spraying or even hosing the leaves in summer will keep them clean, especially in towns, and this also helps to wash away insect pests.

There are two pests which quite frequently attack bay trees; the first is scale insect. These tiny yellowish-brown scales feed on the sap of the plant, collecting mainly on the under surface of the leaves and also on the stems. They excrete a sticky substance called honeydew which encourages a black fungus to grow on the leaves. This also happens on the upper surface so is easily seen, but its cause not always recognized. Both the mould and the scales can be removed by carefully sponging each leaf with soapy water. Unfortunately the eggs left by the scale insect may remain and hatch out, so it may be necessary to spray the plant with an insecticide. I prefer a pyrethrum-based spray so that the leaves can be used almost at once. Malathion is more effective, and a second spray after three weeks is recommended. In this case the leaves will be poisonous for at least four days after spraying and the instructions on the label should be followed

Another increasingly common pest is the bay sucker. Both the adult insects and their larvae (young) feed on the leaves and cause the edges to curl over and become yellow and deformed. It is best to cut off and burn all these leaves or shoots as soon as you see them. If the infestation is very bad you may have to resort to a systemic insecticide, but again the leaves will be poisonous for some while.

Watch out also for tiny caterpillars which may spin two leaves together with a web and feed unnoticed between the two. These are easily removed by hand.

Your tree may well escape all these pests and I am not in any way trying to deter you from growing bay, which is such a valuable flavouring herb for the cook and such a decorative feature in the garden or as a tub plant. It is a slow-growing tree and so it is worth buying a plant at least 30 to 60cm (1 to 2ft) high to start off with. The tiny specimens sometimes sold as 'kitchen bays', though attractive little indoor plants, hardly supply enough flavouring leaves for even one

Bergamot (Monarda didyma)

person. However, bay can be grown by indoor gardeners though it will enjoy a spell outdoors in summer if possible. New plants can be raised from cuttings but these are slow and rather difficult to root. Heel cuttings are taken in midsummer and usually need bottom heat for success.

Bay will give you fresh leaves all the year round. If you need to dry them, cut the leaves from the stems as available and lay them on a rack or nylon netting in the usual way. Leafy sprays can also be hung to dry in a dark airy place.

CARAWAY (*Carum carvi*)

Caraway is one of the many herbs which belong botanically to the *Umbelliferae* family. The flower heads are called umbels and do in fact resemble umbrellas with the flower stalks as spokes and the flowers forming a rounded canopy. The umbels of caraway are white and grow about 45cm (18in) high. It grows wild through Europe to northern India and is occasionally found naturalized in Britain.

Being a biennial or sometimes perennial and grown chiefly for its seeds, these must be sown a whole year or more before you expect to harvest them. Early spring sowing is usually advised, though later sowings can be successful in some districts. The soil should be well drained and the position must be sunny. It is important to sow seed directly into the ground so that no transplanting is necessary, and the seedlings should be thinned out when about 5cm (2in) high leaving them eventually 15 to 20cm (6 to 8in) apart. These thinnings, and also fresh leaves when available, can be used for flavouring and in salads. The plants should be in flower the following midsummer and the seeds ready for harvesting about a month later, just before they are ready to drop. At this stage cut the stems and dry the heads.

If you have plants to spare you can dig them up in winter and use the roots. All this is only worth while though if you have space, and are especially keen to have home-grown seeds. Alternatively you can buy seeds from the stores if you like the very distinctive flavour.

CHERVIL (*Anthriscus cerefolium*)

Chervil is a native of eastern Europe and is sometimes found naturalized in waste places in Britain. It has the typical clusters of tiny flowers of its near relation the cow parsley of hedgerows. However, most flower heads should be cut off or the plant will produce few if any leaves and die off after seeding.

Chervil is not the easiest herb to grow as it likes a well-drained but damp soil. Choose a semi-shady place for the spring sowing where the plants are less likely to dry out in summer sunshine, and you must of course water if necessary. As with so many seedlings of this family (*Umbelliferae*), they resent being transplanted and should be sown where they are to mature, and the seedlings thinned to about 15cm (6in) apart when about 5cm (2in) high. The seeds can be sown in rows 30cm (1ft) apart in the vegetable garden or in pots and window boxes.

You can start cutting from 6 to 8 weeks after sowing, and only cut the outside leaves at first to allow the central shoots to develop. When the plants are growing well they can be cut right across and will renew themselves from the base. If you leave some plants in the row to develop flowers and seeds you should have a new generation of plants to cut during the winter. Also, if gentle summer shade has been provided by other plants which lose their leaves in autumn there will be more sunshine for the winter crop. Some people make several sowings during spring and summer and one in late summer to provide supplies through the winter. It can be protected with cloches in cold districts.

Chervil is not usually recommended for drying as the delicate foliage wilts very quickly after cutting. It can, however, be frozen successfully.

Given the right conditions chervil grows well in pots and window boxes but it is difficult to keep up a supply, and several sowings will have to be made.

CHIVES (*Allium schoenoprasum*)

Occasionally found growing wild in limestone districts of western England and Wales, chives are one of the most rewarding herbs to grow. Belonging to the onion family, they have much smaller, rush-like hollow leaves growing in tufts with only the tiniest suggestion of a bulb at the base. It is the leaves which are used for their mild onion flavour. Chives grow best where the soil is damp and rich in humus and soon become thin and weak if there is not enough sun. They are particularly suitable as an edging to the herb or vegetable garden.

Chives can be grown from seed but most people save time by buying plants or receiving them as gifts from gardening friends. In good soil they increase rapidly and will need dividing in three years or less. You can divide every year if you need extra plants. The best time for this is in spring or autumn, replanting a small ·handful about 5cm (2in) across and allowing 25 to 30cm (10 to 12in) between the new clumps. An edging to a path can soon be made in this way. Cut the clumps frequently to about 5cm (2in) from the ground to encourage new growth. If you allow the plants to flower you will have fewer leaves but they look very pretty and can be used to decorate your salads.

Chives are sometimes attacked by greenfly especially if the soil is too dry. Derris or pyrethrum dust sprinkled into the wet leaves is quick and effective. Cats, though not usually considered as pests, can become addicted to chives and create a quite different problem!

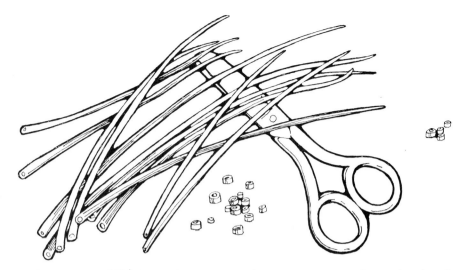

Chives are difficult to dry successfully as they quickly shrivel and lose flavour. Commercially they can be freeze dried which gives excellent results and you can also freeze them yourself.

Window boxes and pots planted with chives sometimes give disappointing results. This is often due to an insufficient supply of soil. With pots I find 18cm (7in) across is the minimum for success. Other causes of failure are a poor potting mixture, or allowing the soil to get too dry.

Chives die down completely in autumn if left in the garden, but you can dig them up before this, plant in pots, cut back to 5cm (2in) high and bring into a greenhouse or sunny window sill. You can extend the season for a while but I have never succeeded in keeping them going for long. It is, however, well worth keeping pot-grown plants in a cold frame in winter to encourage early spring growth.

The Welsh onion (*Allium fistulosum*) and the ever-ready onion, sometimes called onion green, form clumps and tufts similar to chives but have more vigorous growth and a stronger onion flavour. They can be used in the same way as chives and the leaves are even available in winter. They can be grown from seed and are also easily divided.

The giant form of chives growing about 25cm (10in) high has leaves too coarse for eating but is decorative in the herb garden.

CORIANDER (*Coriandrum sativum*)
Coriander was probably the first herb to reach Britain from southern Europe. It is sometimes found naturalized in waste places as it is hardier than most Mediterranean plants. The dark green glossy leaves are attractively shaped and divided and much used in Eastern cooking. Pretty flat clusters of mauve or white flowers appear in midsummer on 45-cm (18-in) stems. Coriander is an annual and the seeds should be sown in spring where the plants are to grow. This could be towards the front of a herb bed or in a row in the vegetable garden. The soil should be well drained and full sun is neces-

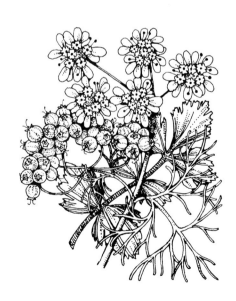

sary to ripen the seed. You will need to thin out the seedlings leaving them about 15cm (6in) apart. Fresh young leaves can be used for flavouring and make a pretty decoration if used in the same way as parsley leaves.

The heads should be cut as soon as the first seeds begin to ripen and drying completed under cover. Before the seeds are fully ripe their smell and taste is very unpleasant and the Greeks likened it to the smell of bugs. They named the plant 'Kŏriandron' from *koris* meaning 'a bug'.

A herb then for your seedlist though sometimes available as a pot-grown plant if you forget to buy the seed in time.

COSTMARY (*Chrysanthemum balsamita*)

Costmary is a native of Asia Minor, the Caucasus and Iran, but has been a herb garden plant certainly since the 16th century and was formerly used to flavour ale, hence its other name — alecost. It is dedicated to St Mary Magdalene, though the Latin *costus amarus* means a bitter shrub.

It is rather an untidy plant but well worth growing in the border or herb garden. The leaves are an attractive grey-green colour but the flower stems which grow sometimes 1m (3ft) high have rather insignificant clusters of small yellow flowers.

Costmary can be grown from seed but as you will probably only need one plant this is hardly worth while. Being a perennial it will come up each year and usually spreads quickly and needs dividing in spring. The new plants are best in a group with about 45cm (18in) between each plant. Pot-grown plants are available for spring or autumn planting.

Young leaves are available throughout the year, though mainly in spring and summer. Try costmary as a substitute for mint when the latter has disappeared in winter.

Flowers and leaves can be dried in the usual way if required for the non-culinary uses suggested in the A to Z.

CUMIN (*Cuminum cyminum*)

Cumin is a half-hardy annual and native of Egypt. Its feathery leaves resemble fennel, though it is a less vigorous plant and the rather dull flowers are pink or white. It is seldom grown in Britain, partly because the seed is only obtainable from specialist nurseries, and partly because our summers are not always warm enough to ripen the seed for harvesting. However, if you want to try something different and enjoy taking a chance, this is the herb for you.

In most districts it is best to sow the seed in the greenhouse in spring and then transfer the seedlings with as large a ball of soil as possible to the open garden when danger of frost is past. Like so many annual herbs it resents disturbance, so you may have as much success by sowing directly into the garden in late spring. Well-drained soil is necessary and as warm and sunny a place as you can find. Thin the seedlings to 15cm (6in) apart.

Cumin is grown only for its seeds which should be ready for harvesting in midsummer. Cut the stems just before the seeds are fully ripe and dry in the usual way. The seeds have an unpleasant taste before they are fully ripe.

DILL (*Anethum graveolens*)

Dill is a hardy annual from southern Europe and western Asia, which is closely related to the perennial fennel. For this reason it is best not to grow the two plants near each other or they will 'intermarry' and you will get hybrid seedlings, unless you remove the flower heads. It has the typical bluish-green feathery leaves and yellowish-green clusters of flowers produced by its taller relation.

Dill sometimes only grows about 30cm (1ft) high but is taller

in moist soil. Given the right conditions it grows quickly and easily, but if the soil is too dry it soon produces tiny unproductive flower heads and dies off. On the other hand dill will not grow well in heavy, badly drained soil, and it will be impossible to get the fine crumbly texture necessary for seed sowing. So, as with many herbs, a well-drained soil and sunny position will give you the best hope for success, and you must, of course, water in dry weather.

Sow the seeds where you wish the plants to grow. Thin out the seedlings gradually so that each plant has room to grow, leaving them eventually about 23cm (9in) apart. A first sowing must be made in spring if you want the plants to set seed, but successive sowings through the summer will give you leaves to cut for flavouring and garnishing.

Greenfly and a similar insect called leaf hopper sometimes attack dill, especially if the plants are growing too thickly or the roots are dry. Spray with pyrethrum if necessary.

Drying the leaves is unfortunately difficult owing to the fragile nature of the leaves, but they will freeze well. Seed heads for drying should be cut before the seeds are ready to fall.

Dill is a useful and pretty foliage plant to grow in pots on a windowsill or in window boxes among other plants.

ELDER (*Sambucus nigra*)

Elder is a native shrub of British hedgerows, particularly on chalky soils, and has been revered for centuries as a magical plant giving protection against witches and other evils.

Seedlings often appear uninvited in country gardens as the birds enjoy the berries as much as we do. It is a coarse-growing plant up to 9m (30ft) high in the wild but it can be kept much smaller by pruning the previous year's growth back to a few buds in early spring.

However, it is not usually planted in a prominent position in the garden unless one of the more attractive yellow- or cut-leaved varieties are grown (see page 46).

Its stems are hollow and were used in the past to make a harp-like musical instrument called a sambuca.

It likes a damp, preferably chalky soil and will give you most flowers and berries where it has sun for at least part of the day. Being a hardy deciduous shrub (losing its leaves in winter), it can be moved or planted any time in late autumn and winter. No special preparation of the soil is usually necessary but I like to give all my shrubs and trees a good start, as described on page 44. This will be especially valuable if your soil is light and easily becomes dry in summer.

Cuttings of current years growth about 45cm (18in) long can be cut off and rooted easily in the open ground in late autumn after the leaves have fallen.

Elder is sometimes badly infested by blackfly in early spring as the new growth develops. This is usually controlled by one spray of derris or pyrethrum, though a second spray is sometimes necessary after a week or two.

The large clusters of elder flowers are best cut when all the buds are fully open. They can be used fresh or dried. Drying must be carried out carefully with the heads lying on nylon netting and the stalks pointing upwards, each head separated to avoid discoloration. The usual dark airy place suggested for drying herbs will be necessary.

The berries are cut in late summer to early autumn as they ripen. Country dwellers are usually lucky enough to find all the flowers and berries they need without bothering to grow a bush themselves.

FENNEL (*Foeniculum vulgare*)
Fennel is found growing wild on sea cliffs in Wales, and from Norfolk southwards in England, on cliffs and sometimes in waste places. It has been grown for centuries as a herb garden plant. A tall perennial, sometimes up to 2m (6ft) high, it has bluish-green, finely divided leaves and yellowish-green flower heads which are also quite attractive.

It is easy to grow, even flourishing in heavier soils, but prefers light, well-drained conditions, and resents dryness at the roots unless it is well established. Like its near relation dill, it does well in chalky or alkaline soils.

If you want to harvest seeds you must grow it in a really sunny place and sow the seed in early spring. For a supply of fresh leaves, later sowings can be made and the plants can be grown in less sunny positions. By frequent cutting the plants may be kept to about 45cm (18in) high, or, alternatively, allowed to grow up and give an attractive background effect in the border. Sow the seeds where the plants are required to grow and gradually thin out the seedlings to leave them about 30cm (1ft) apart. Pot-grown plants are usually available at nurseries and garden centres in spring and sometimes also in autumn. Once established, fennel can be increased by division and this will become necessary in any case after three or four years. By this time you may also have a forest of fennel seedlings!

Fennel is sometimes attacked by greenfly, especially in dry weather.

The leaves are not recommended for drying as the flavour is easily lost, but with a freezer you can preserve both the stems and leaves. The seeds are also difficult to dry; they must be cut when still light green, but the low temperature needed for storing makes them liable to become mouldy.

The so-called black fennel, which is in fact a pretty bronze colour, has all the same culinary uses as ordinary fennel and is well worth growing as a decorative garden plant (see page 48). Either one can be grown as an outdoor pot plant and both do well in a town atmosphere. If you keep them cut back as described above, the ultimate height will be no problem. Plants may also be bought or potted up in autumn and brought indoors or into the greenhouse for a supply of fresh leaves in winter.

Many people are confused by seeing fennel for sale in greengrocers, with swollen leafstalks, resembling a white bulb, with a small tuft of green at the top. This is Florence fennel, a vegetable and salad plant popular in France and Italy. The British climate is not normally warm enough to grow it well, but seed is obtainable and you could try it out.

GARLIC (*Allium sativum*)
A native of central Asia and cultivated in the Middle East and Mediterranean area for many centuries BC. It was fed to the workers on the pyramids, the Egyptians no doubt realizing its medicinal value in keeping a healthy labour force.

As garlic is grown commercially in many warmer countries, such as Spain and Rumania, most people find it cheaper and easier to buy the cloves from a grocer. The last time I grew them was during the

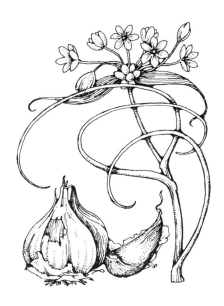

1939–45 war. However, if you have time and space in the vegetable garden you may like to try growing your own.

Garlic grows from a bulb which splits before lifting time into a number of small bulbs called cloves. In milder parts of Britain the bulblets or cloves are planted both in spring and autumn 5cm (2in) deep and 15cm (6in) apart in rows 30cm (12in) apart. In colder districts plant only in spring. To develop they will need sun and a good, deeply dug, moist soil not firmed too hard before planting. When the tops yellow and die off in midsummer the bulbs are lifted and hung up in bunches to finish the drying process under cover. The separated cloves can also be used for replanting.

There are interesting records of garlic preventing and even curing the disease of peach leaf curl when it is planted underneath the tree, and that it also makes nearby plants more resistant to attack by greenfly. Evidently an excretion from the roots has an effect on the sap of other plants. Useful to have around, though you would need a lot of garlic to eliminate all pests and diseases!

GERANIUM (*Pelargonium spp*)
Many of us grow hardy geraniums in our gardens and several are native to Britain; but, confusingly, the pelargonium is commonly called a 'geranium', and these are half-hardy plants introduced from South Africa during the 18th century. The large colourful flowers of the zonal pelargoniums were favourites of the Victorians who used their elaborate greenhouses and conservatories to protect the plants in winter. They also loved the scented-leaved 'geraniums' which are the ones we grow for flavouring, and particularly for pot-pourri where the scent is strongly retained in the dried leaves. These leaves are often attractively shaped and sometimes deeply cut and divided as in the 'lemon-scented geranium'.

Most people start by buying a pot plant in early summer. This plant will have been grown in a greenhouse and it is as well to be sure it is hardened off properly before planting in the garden when all danger of frost is over. Geraniums do best in slightly alkaline or neutral soils and those which are well drained. They enjoy full sun, but if you are growing them mainly for their leaves, an open position with sun for only part of the day will be quite adequate. The flowers of the scented-leaved varieties are delicate shades of mauve, pink and white.

In late summer the plants must be dug up from the garden and potted up separately; or several plants may be put together in a larger container of soil, and kept in a frost-free place for the winter. Large plants can be shaken free of soil and actually hung up from their roots to dry off. Whichever method you use there may well be casualties and I like to take several cuttings of each plant in mid- to late summer. These young plants can easily be kept through the winter in a frost-free greenhouse or sunny window and will be ideal for planting the following summer as already described. Cuttings can be taken in spring from the plants you have successfully over-wintered. These will root easily.

Fresh leaves are best to use for flavouring but leaves can be cut at any time during the summer and dried carefully in the usual way.

'Geraniums' are ideal pot and window box plants for patios and balconies and a must for the indoor gardener with a sunny room or windowsill.

HORSERADISH (*Cochlearia armoracia*)
Though native to southern Europe, after its introduction in the late Middle Ages horseradish soon naturalized itself in Britain and can be found wild in waste ground in England and Wales, though it is rare in Scotland and Ireland. It is a very coarse, vigorous plant which has stems of small white flowers growing up to 1·25m (4ft) high, and large dock-like leaves.

Though it will grow in poor soil in the wild, in order to encourage more fleshy and profitable roots we need to plant it in rich, moist, but well-drained soil and preferably in the sun. This sort of position is precious in a garden and as horseradish will soon swamp and kill off its near neighbours it should be planted in as isolated a place as possible, or not at all! Like a number of weeds, such as dandelion and bindweed, it can propagate itself from small pieces of root left in the ground when you try to dig it up. On the other hand these pieces of root, or thongs, are a ready means of propagating the plant. You may decide you have just the place for it.

For really good results the soil should be dug 60cm (2ft) deep and manure incorporated about 30cm (1ft) down. The usual planting time is spring but it can also be done in autumn. You can buy a pot-grown plant, or thongs about 20cm (8in) long. These are planted with the thickest end upward, just below soil level. By digging up and clearing the bed entirely every year or two you will prevent the invasion of the remainder of the garden! In this case the roots can be stored in damp sand, otherwise you can lift them as required. They soon lose their valuable properties if allowed to dry, although commercial drying methods can be successful.

Horseradish is not recommended for pots, window boxes or indoor growing!

JUNIPER (*Juniperus communis*)

Juniper is one of Britain's few native conifers which used to be commonly found in chalky upland districts and was planted to make arbors and hedges in early gardens. It was considered a magic shrub and was used to ward off devils, spirits and wild animals. The grey-green foliage and stems are strongly aromatic and the berries have been used for their flavour and medicinal value since Tudor times, or possibly earlier. The male and female flowers are on separate plants so you need at least one shrub of each sex planted close together in order to ensure fertilization and the production of berries.

Juniperus communis is difficult to obtain, though other species are listed by many nurseries but their berries should not be used. If you do manage to obtain plants they will grow easily in most soils, especially on chalk and in sun or part shade. The best time for planting is early autumn or spring.

Cuttings can be rooted in sandy soil in a cold frame in early autumn, or seeds may be sown in spring or autumn. Unfortunately these may take a whole year to germinate.

Berries may be two to three years ripening on the plants, gradually turning from green to black, and you must not be tempted to harvest the green berries. When ripe they can be dried in a warm dark place and kept not longer than a year or they lose their flavour and aroma. You may well decide to buy your berries from

the stores or collect them in the wild, if you are lucky enough to find them. The berries are, in the words of Thomas Tusser in 1557, 'To be bought with the Pense'.

LEMON BALM (*Melissa officinalis*)

Lemon balm is a native of southern Europe but was an early introduction to Britain and has become naturalized in the southern counties. This is not surprising as it grows easily from seed. Its strongly aromatic, lemon-scented leaves made it a favourite herb for strewing on medieval and Tudor floors. It is a leafy perennial about 60cm (2ft) high and its spikes of tiny white fowers, though very attractive to bees, are not any asset to the garden picture. It will grow in any soil, though on moist and rich soils you will get larger leaves in greater numbers.

Plant in autumn or spring, the latter being preferable in very cold districts and here the plants will benefit from a light mulch of peat or leafmould in autumn. Plants are easily obtainable from nurseries and garden centres and once established you will have no difficulty in increasing your stock by dividing the roots in spring or autumn. The plants will no doubt seed themselves and if you want even more plants you can root soft cuttings easily in summer.

Greenfly seem to like the taste of lemon balm and cut sprays for immediate use or drying should be carefully washed if necessary.

Fresh leaves can be used for flavouring throughout the summer as suggested in the A to Z. The stems are usually cut for drying as the flower buds develop, but several cuttings can be made. The usual dark airy place is necessary and artificial heat should be avoided. Freezing is easier if you have this useful aid to preservation.

There is an attractive golden-variegated form which is also lemon scented, but I grow the

entirely golden leaved form only for its decorative effect in the garden (see page 48).

LEMON VERBENA (*Lippia citriodora*)

Lemon verbena is a native of Chile and only introduced to Britain in the late 18th century when the wealthy had heated greenhouses to keep the plants in during the winter. It is, however, hardy in the milder counties of the south and west of England and even further north can be grown outside if protected in winter.

It should be planted in the shelter of a south-facing wall and the soil should not be rich or the growth will be soft and more vulnerable to frost. Against a wall it is fairly simple to protect the roots with a mulch of peat and/or straw or bracken and to even make a cage of wire netting about 1m (3ft) high loosely packed with strawy material. Should you have an old window frame or spare 'light' from a garden frame this can be propped against the wall and gives excellent protection to the lower part of the plant. Cuttings root easily, either soft growth in summer or ripened woody shoots in late summer or autumn.

The leaves can be used fresh or dried, their delicious scent and flavour being beautifully retained by drying. Sprays are usually cut in midsummer when the plant is in flower, as the latter also dry well, making it an ideal plant for pot-pourri.

Lemon verbena is often grown in a tub or large pot for which it

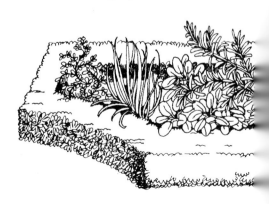

is ideal. Protection in winter is made considerably easier and surer. Bring the plant indoors or into a frost-free greenhouse. Indoor gardeners can also enjoy lemon verbena.

LOVAGE (*Ligusticum officinale*)

Britain has a native lovage (*L. scoticum*) which grows on rocky coasts northward from Northumberland, and the cultivated *L. officinale*, first introduced by the Romans, is also sometimes found as a garden escape. Both plants have the characteristic strong, spicy, celery flavour.

Lovage is a vigorous perennial sometimes growing as much as 2·5m (8ft) high. Its attractively divided leaves are bronze in spring and then become dark green and very glossy. It is an effective 'architectural plant' if you have room for it. The greenish flower heads may be 13 to 15cm (5 to 6in) across and are useful in large flower arrangements, as are the seed heads which follow.

As you will probably only need one plant it might be more sensible to buy this rather than to sow seed. Once it is established you can save your own seed and this is best sown soon after it ripens in late summer. Young seedlings can be transplanted in autumn or spring and you can also divide the fleshy roots in spring. The plants grow best in moist, rich soils in sun or part shade.

Leaves and stems can be used fresh through the summer and if only leaves are required, flower heads should be cut out. Spring

is the best time to dig and use the roots.

Young lovage leaves can be dried in the usual way and also freeze successfully. The seed heads should be cut for drying just before they are fully ripe.

Lovage is a useful herb, though not often seen in gardens.

MARJORAM (*Origanum vulgare* – wild marjoram; *O. onites* – pot marjoram; *O. marjorana* – sweet marjoram)

Wild marjoram is native to Britain, mainly on chalky downland, and is also found widespread in Europe. It is a pretty perennial plant with clusters of tiny mauve flowers and grows from 30 to 60cm (1 to 2ft) high. Unfortunately it does not develop as much flavour in Britain as it does around the Mediterranean where it is called oregano. To add to confusion the Mexicans have the same name for a much more pungent plant – *Lippia graveolens*.

For flavouring, most people prefer to grow pot marjoram, an eastern Mediterranean plant. This is also a perennial and is rather shrubby with pink or white flowers in attractive, more drooping sprays. It does best in the sun and a well-drained soil enriched by compost or leafmould so that the plants do not dry out too easily in summer. As it is a perennial, most people start by buying a plant, but it can also be grown from seed. It is, however, rather slow to germinate and difficult to grow on successfully. Once established it is easy to propagate by separating small rooted pieces in spring, or taking half-ripe cuttings in summer.

Sweet marjoram is very strongly aromatic, perhaps too much so for some people. It is native to southern Europe, northern Africa and western Asia and has to be treated as a half-hardy annual in Britain. You can either buy seed or a pot plant if available. Though naturally a bushy plant about 30cm (1ft) high it sometimes de-

velops a more trailing growth which looks well in a pot. Sow seed in a frame or greenhouse in spring, prick out the seedlings into boxes or peat pots and delay planting in the garden until the danger of frost is over. Where the soil is light, and it is easy to make a fine seedbed, marjoram can be sown directly into the garden in late spring.

Young sprigs can be cut for flavouring throughout the summer months, but the best time for cutting marjorams for drying is just before the flowers fully develop. When dried well the aroma can be retained and even increased, but freezing is usually more reliable.

The marjorams make pretty pot plants and grow well in window boxes. Plants from the garden can also be dug up, potted into good compost, trimmed over, and grown as indoor plants in the winter. In the garden marjorams look well in the front of a border with their bushy mounds of tiny green leaves and pretty flowers. The pretty golden-leaved marjoram is especially attractive and described on page 48.

MINT (*Mentha spp*)

Mint has been grown as a cultivated plant perhaps longer than any other European herb, and probably from Neolithic times. There are at least twelve different mints grown in gardens although many people only know and grow spearmint with its familiar pointed, stemless leaves and attractive spikes of mauve flowers in late summer. This mint has escaped from gardens and become naturalized in the damp places it enjoys. So in the garden, to grow mint well, we need a moist soil enriched with compost or decayed manure and a partially shady place. In the country most new gardeners are given mint by their friends who usually have more than they need. Otherwise pot-grown plants are available from nurseries and garden centres.

Because of its rampant creeping growth many people plant mint in an old bucket or polythene bag, but be sure the bottom is removed or well pierced to allow good drainage. When dividing take the horizontal stems which have several shoots on them and plant 5cm (2in) deep and 15cm (6in) apart. This can be done in spring or autumn. If your soil is at all dry it is better to grow apple mint, a taller-growing plant with rounded hairy leaves. Some people in fact consider the flavour is better than spearmint and it is less likely to suffer from mint rust.

Mint rust first shows in spring as thickened young shoots with tiny orange spots on them. Eventually the leaves become infected and plants should be pulled up and burnt at once. It is possible to

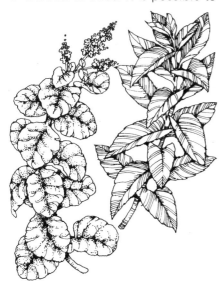

disinfect the roots but if a patch is badly infected I prefer to start again with new roots in another part of the garden. Renewing clumps by dividing and replanting every two or three years will invigorate the plants and make them less likely to succumb to disease.

Mint shoots can be cut throughout the growing season, in fact it is best to keep the plants to about 15cm (6in) to encourage new growths. The best time to cut for drying is just as the plant comes into flower and cut sprigs will freeze well.

Mint can be grown in pots or window boxes, but it is wisest to plant it alone rather than with other less invasive plants. Mint can also be lifted, potted up, cut back to the usual 15cm (6in) and brought indoors or into a heated greenhouse for a winter supply. If too cold the mint will die down as if it were outdoors.

Other mints have less culinary value but are well worth growing if only to pinch and smell as you pass. Eau de Cologne mint is perhaps the most refreshing for this, and pineapple mint has a delicious scent. Both of these are excellent to dry for pot-pourri. Peppermint is mainly used for a refreshing herb tea.

Pennyroyal (*M. pulegium*) was much used medicinally in the past and has a very strong flavour. The scent, however, is particularly refreshing when crushed by hand or foot. It is used as a creeping plant for an aromatic lawn and has tiny leaves and pretty spikes of mauve flowers. Its name *pulegium* — from *pulex*, the latin for flea — reminds us that it was used against this noxious insect. It was also valued for disinfecting polluted drinking water.

My favourite mint is the beautiful white-variegated apple mint with felted leaves, this is also of culinary use but is included in my list of decorative herbs on page 48. Mints have as many varied uses as any herbs we grow.

NASTURTIUM (*Tropaeolum majus* and *T. minus*)

Many people grow nasturtiums without realizing their culinary value and their health-giving vitamin C content. The nasturtium first came to Britain in the late 16th century from its native Peru and the West Indies and was soon a popular salad herb, particularly at a time when salads were more often decorated with flowers which were also edible.

Nasturtiums are in every seed catalogue and there is no problem

in growing them, though they flower best in sunny positions and poor dry soil. If, however, you are mainly concerned with a good supply of leaves, dig in some garden compost or peat before sowing the seed, so that the soil does not dry out so easily, and a semishady place would be suitable. Nasturtiums are annuals and although listed as hardy they should certainly not be sown before late spring. The large seeds can be pressed into the soil 1cm ($\frac{1}{2}$in) deep where you want them to grow. There are climbing varieties which can be trained up a twiggy support or over a bank, and really dwarf varieties for the front of borders. The Jewel strain is very pretty with the flowers held well above the leaves, a good choice if you are mainly concerned with a colourful display. I prefer single to double flowers but there are also semi-trailing Gleam hybrids which are scented as well as double flowered. (See also page 50.) Many people refuse to grow nasturtiums because they are attacked by blackfly which often cluster thickly underneath the lower leaves. Badly affected leaves should be removed and the plants sprayed with derris or pyrethrum. I never find these blackfly spread to other plants, in fact nasturtiums are said to protect nearby plants from insect attack.

Leaves and flowers can be cut as available during the summer and the best time for cutting the leaves for drying is just before flowering, when the vitamin C content is highest. Many people neglect the culinary value of their nasturtiums and forget that the young buds and young green seeds can be pickled and used as a substitute for capers. They make ideal pot plants for outdoor windowsills, patios, balconies and window boxes.

PARSLEY (*Petroselinum crispum*)
Parsley has been grown as a cultivated herb for so long that its

origin is obscure, but it probably first grew wild in southern Europe and was brought to Britain by the Romans who certainly used it in their cooking. It became a favourite medieval flavouring herb.

Parsley is a biennial and usually runs to seed the year after it is sown. Pot-grown plants are available from nurseries and garden centres in spring, but as most people use a lot of parsley it is much more economical to sow your own seed. There are several varieties to choose from, some having very finely cut and crinkled leaves, called moss curled, others with plain, fern like leaves, which are usually hardiest in winter. I grow two varieties: Paramount Imperial Curled which is curled but also very hardy and does not easily run to seed; I also like to grow a fern-leaved form, usually called French parsley, which is extremely hardy, its pretty bright green leaves seem to even enjoy the snow and frost and the flavour is also good. Unfortunately the leaves resemble a poisonous weed called, appropriately, fools parsley (*Aethusa cynapium*), so watch out for this carefully.

Some people find parsley difficult to grow and many superstitions surround it. Being slow to germinate it is said to go nine times to the devil before it will come up, and you must sow it on Good Friday in the form of a cross.

The secret is to have a good rich soil, where compost or preferably well-rotted manure has been dug in fairly recently. This will both feed the plants and provide moisture as they grow. Parsley succeeds in both sun or part shade. Germination can take five to six weeks but this, I find, can be reduced to two weeks by soaking the seed overnight or for up to 24 hours in water which should preferably be tepid to start. The seeds tend to stick together after soaking but mixed with a little dry sand it is not too difficult to separate them. Others recommend pouring

very hot water over the seed after it has been sown.

Parsley can only be transplanted when it is very small so it is usually sown into the garden where you want it to grow. Alternatively, you can sometimes buy a pot of tiny seedlings which is very good value if you prick them out carefully into good soil and make sure they never dry out, at least until they are established. Also on sale are pots containing only one plant ready to transfer to the garden, window box or larger pot. The first sowing in the garden can be made in spring and further sowings up to midsummer if you wish. If your soil outside is too heavy, or there is a period of drought, it is worth sowing your parsley in a seed box. Given bottom heat, germination will be speeded up and seedlings can then be pricked out into peat pots and transferred to the garden later without any further root disturbance. Seedlings in the garden must be gradually thinned out so that they are finally left about 20cm (8in) apart (rather less if your soil is not very rich).

When the plants are growing well the older leaves may be cut a few at a time and this encourages more growth from the centre. An occasional liquid feed will speed them along. During the winter it pays to cover at least a few plants with a cloche so that you have a source of supply during frosty weather. The following spring some of your plants will start sending up flowerheads which should be nipped out or the plants will seed and die off. The quality of the leaves is not so good the second year and it is wise to make a new sowing in spring in order to ensure a continuous supply, and a further sowing in midsummer if required. Watch out for greenfly, especially during a dry spell, and you will find that rabbits have a special liking for parsley and nibble them right down so that the growing point dies and you have to

start again. Apart from wire netting I know of no sure way of keeping them off.

It is difficult to retain the flavour in dried parsley so freeze it if possible, though it is an easy matter (compared with many herbs) to keep a fresh supply throughout the year. Parsley is ideal for growing outdoors in pots and window boxes, remembering the need for a rich soil and never of course letting the pots dry out. It is also the easiest herb for the indoor gardener who can keep a supply going the whole year by making at least two sowings. I find the French or fern-leaved parsley does particularly well and looks very pretty in a pot. Small plants from the garden can also be potted up and brought indoors for convenient use in winter.

The Hamburg parsley is not often grown. This has a tap root rather like a parsnip and is used more as a vegetable. It is sown in the garden in spring, also needs a rich moist soil and grows well in the shade. Roots can be lifted as required in winter or stored as you would other root vegetables. The leaves are very hardy and can be used throughout the winter from plants left in the ground.

Everyone should grow parsley, it is a rich source of minerals and vitamin C and has such a pretty leaf that it is often used as an edging plant beside a path and is sometimes recommended to grow with rose bushes. It certainly does well there, partly I suspect, due to the fertilizing and mulch of manure which rose beds usually get in spring. However, do be careful not to spray your roses with some noxious fluid against pests or diseases and so temporarily make your parsley inedible and poisonous.

PURSLANE (*Portulaca oleracea*)
Grown since early times for its magical, medicinal and culinary uses, purslane is seldom seen in herb gardens in Britain, though you sometimes see its more flamboyant relations with brilliant pink and purple flowers. It is popular, however, in Europe and seed is available here, though it may be difficult to obtain the attractive golden-leaved form. It is these small fleshy leaves which are used, the stems being quite hard.

Purslane enjoys a well-drained but rich soil in full sun and will need watering in dry weather. It is only a moderately hardy annual and best treated as half hardy. An outdoor sowing in spring should be covered with cloches (or, alternatively, wait until late spring). Subsequent thinning to 23cm (9in) apart is recommended. Several sowings can be made as purslane is ready for cutting within two months of sowing. As it is a spreading plant patches are really better than rows, and it makes an attractive ground-cover plant among herbs or in the vegetable garden.

The fleshy leaves are best picked off separately, using only the young ones for salads and the older ones for cooking. They are succulent and, therefore, unsuitable for drying, but they can be frozen successfully. There is no reason why purslane should not be grown as an outdoor pot plant or in a window box but it would be wise not to try sowing it in an already established box of herbs

where the seedlings would become weak and drawn.

ROSEMARY (*Rosmarinus officinalis*)
If forced to choose only one herb for their garden, many people would choose rosemary. Growing wild in the Mediterranean area from sea level to mountain hillsides it is thought that the Romans introduced it to Britain, but it may well have been lost and reintroduced later. The bush itself is attractive with its small, thin, dark green leaves which are white on the reverse side and sometimes give the plant a greyish appearance. Its tiny mauve flowers sometimes open in midwinter and are a welcome source of food for the earliest bees. There are various forms and named varieties of rosemary some with more upright growth and others with deeper blue flowers described more fully on pages 46 and 47.

Rosemary is doubtfully hardy in colder areas and is usually planted against a south wall where it can be partly trained upward and also allowed to fall forwards in a natural and graceful way.

Although rosemary roots easily from cuttings, most people buy a pot-grown plant in spring and plant it in prepared soil. If the plant is small, little if any cutting will be possible during the first season and if you want upright growth it is best not to cut the central growing shoot unless the plant is very thin and 'leggy'. In later years some pruning may be necessary after flowering in order to keep a good shape, and if a plant has completely outgrown its position large pieces can be cut out even to ground level in spring.

After flowering a healthy rosemary bush will make considerable new growth and when these shoots are beginning to harden at the base in midsummer cuttings can be taken with or without a heel. Cuttings can in fact be taken right into the early autumn and I

have even successfully rooted them in a sheltered spot outdoors in late autumn.

Fresh rosemary leaves and shoots can be cut at any time from established plants but the best growths to cut for drying are the younger but maturing shoots in later summer. They will lose colour if the temperature is too high.

Rosemary makes an ideal plant for a pot or tub, especially in cold districts where it can more easily be given protection in winter. Indoor gardens can also have small rosemary plants but they are really best outdoors in summer and only in cool light rooms in winter.

SAGE (*Salvia officinalis*)
Another Mediterranean herb probably introduced to Britain by the Romans and no doubt also brought across from French to English monasteries during the Middle Ages. The medicinal value of sage was recognized in early times and it was an important physic herb.

Sage is a shrubby plant with grey-green leaves which become attractively silver especially in a dry summer. The leaves have a texture which Gerard vividly describes in his Herbal of 1597, 'like in roughnes to woollen cloth threadbare'. These leaves remain throughout the winter. It grows particularly well in light chalky soils but is one of the few herbs which will grow successfully on heavy clay soil provided there is reasonable drainage. The main requirement is a sunny position.

Most people start by buying a pot-grown plant in the spring and although it quickly establishes itself there will not be much to cut the first year. After this, fairly frequent cutting will keep the plant bushy. Leggy plants can be pruned back in spring but may not break again from very old wood. In fact sage really needs replacing by cuttings after three or four years. I like to take these cuttings a year before I need them so that the plants are maturing before I remove the parents. Some people earth up old plants in spring so that shoots produce roots into the soil and can be detached. I find that prunings at this time will root easily in water, particularly the younger shoots, about 15cm (6in) long. They will, in fact, root right through the summer and autumn in a sheltered, semi-shady spot outdoors, without even any glass protection. The broad-leaved sage seldom flowers in this country and must be increased by cuttings or layers, but the narrow-leaved form, which is not considered to have such good flavour, can be grown from seed.

Sage is a remarkably trouble-free plant, will survive long periods of drought and is seldom if ever attacked by pest or disease. Leaves or sprays are available for cutting from established plants throughout the spring and summer and there is usually enough for a winter supply unless the weather is particularly severe.

If you wish to dry sage, you can cut twice, both in early and midsummer. It must be dried slowly on a frame or hung up in bunches in a cool airy place. Sage is an ideal plant for outdoor pots and window boxes and can be kept small by frequently nipping out the growing points. I have not tried it as an indoor pot plant but it would

no doubt survive for a while.

There are several particularly decorative forms of sage such as the purple-leaved and golden-variegated kinds which are described on pages 47 and 48.

SALAD BURNET (*Sanguisorba minor*)

Salad burnet (sometimes confusingly called *Poterium sanguisorba*) is a native British plant found on chalky downland and is much appreciated by sheep, particularly in winter. Its charming leaves are described by Turner in his Herball of 1551, 'It has two little leaves like onto the wings of birds, standing out as the bird setteth her wings out as she intendeth to flye'. Its flowers are like little round balls which gradually turn from green to red.

Being a perennial it is usually sold as a pot-grown plant but can also be started from seed. It can be planted in spring or autumn and existing plants can also be divided at these times. Although enjoying chalky soil, salad burnet will flourish in a wide range of soils and in sun or part shade, where it makes pretty ground cover between shrubs.

Use only the young tender leaves for their delicate cucumber flavour, and encourage more new growth by keeping the plant to about 15cm (6in) high and pre-

venting it from flowering.

There is no need to dry or freeze the leaves as they are available all the year round and even continue growing in the winter in any but the very coldest districts.

It is one of the prettiest and easiest herbs to grow in a pot outdoors and I find it looks best alone rather than mixed with other plants in window boxes. Brought indoors it would tend to get leggy and unattractive but it could be tried for a limited time. Every gardener should have salad burnet.

SAVORY (*Satureja montana* — winter savory; *S. hortensis* — summer savory)

Both savories are Mediterranean plants which were used in Roman cooking and favoured by medieval cooks for their strong flavour before spices from the East Indies were in common use.

Winter savory is a dwarf evergreen shrub which will only grow about 30cm (1ft) high and it would be worthy of a place in the garden even without its aromatic and culinary use. From midsummer sometimes on into the autumn it will be covered with tiny, usually white flowers and is much visited by bees. Pot plants of winter savory can be bought in spring and planted in light, well-drained, rather poor soil in full sun where they will be tough plants best able

to withstand the winter. If you want a lot of plants, say for an edging or tiny hedge, seeds can be sown in boxes or in the ground in spring in the usual way. Otherwise propagation is easy by dividing plants in spring or taking small heel cuttings in spring or summer. It can also be layered. The flavour of savory is strong, and only a tiny amount is needed in cooking.

Summer savory is an annual and requires a richer soil but also needs the sun. Seed should be sown outdoors in late spring, thinning the seedlings to leave them about 15cm (6in) apart. It grows about the same height as winter savory but is more upright and the flavour more delicate. Summer savory is cut for drying just before flowering. Dry it either by hanging it in bunches, or placing it on netted trays in the usual way. As winter savory is available all the year round in most districts there is no necessity to dry it. You can always cover with a cloche if the weather is severe. Either savory can be grown in outdoor pots and window boxes in summer and winter savory might be worth bringing indoors if you have it in a pot. I find the plants keep healthier in a cold frame. I strongly recommend them; particularly winter savory which is so easy to grow.

SORREL (*Rumex scutatus* – French sorrel)

The sorrels are smaller relations of the dock and the British native sorrel (*R. acetosa*) is a common weed, especially on more acid soils. The French sorrel has a milder and more pleasant flavour and is also found naturalized in places. It is native to southern Europe and much more widely used on the continent and in France as its name suggests. Grow it in sun or part shade. A light, rich soil which does not dry out easily will suit it best. It is one of the few herbs preferring an acid rather than an alkaline soil.

Although only a few leaves are required when used fresh, it reduces considerably, like spinach, when cooked, so several plants will probably be needed. Seed can be sown outdoors in spring where the plants are to grow, preferably in a row in the vegetable garden. Thin the seedlings to 38 to 45cm (15 to 18in). You can also start by buying a plant in spring or autumn and in later years you can divide and replant at these times. Green 60-cm (2-ft) high flower spikes will appear in summer and these should be removed or the leaves will become tough and unpalatable. You can start to cut the fresh green leaves when the plants are growing well and have a cluster of four or five leaves. Leaves for winter use can be cut for drying or freezing just before flowering time.

Sorrel is an easy herb, growing like the weed it actually is, but it is certainly not to be despised on this account.

SWEET CICELY (*Myrrhis odorata*)

As beautiful a plant as its name suggests, sweet Cicely is a native plant in the more mountainous parts of northern England and southern Scotland and in similar areas of southern Europe. It has finely divided, pale green fern-like leaves and is a stately plant growing slowly to an ultimate height of about 1·25m (4ft) with flat heads of small white flowers which are followed by seeds (botanically, in fact, fruits) which are surprisingly

large, about 1cm ($\frac{1}{2}$in) long, green at first and darkening to brown as they ripen. It is usual to start by buying a plant which, when established, will supply many self sown seedlings if the fruits are allowed to ripen on the plant. It does best in moist semi-shade and quickly wilts if the soil becomes too dry. It unfortunately also wilts quickly when cut, otherwise it would give ideal material for flower arranging. Roots may be divided in spring or autumn, but as it dies down so late in the year early spring is preferable; the leaves begin to shoot again in late winter. The leaves and leaf stalks are mainly used fresh as the soft leaves are difficult to dry. The flowers, however, are sometimes dried for potpourri, and they need to be cut in any case if the leaves are required to give their best flavour. Where seeds are allowed to form they can be dried in the usual way but are very hard and must be finely crushed before using. The roots are also edible, but you would need a lot of plants to be able to sacrifice them in this way.

Sweet Cicely makes a pretty pot plant even when young, and each year will need a larger pot eventually about 30cm (1ft) across to give it the deep, moist root run it enjoys.

In the garden I plant it in the semi-shade among ferns, hostas and hellebores rather than with the herbs which are so largely sun loving.

TARRAGON (*Artemisia dracunculus*)

Tarragon is related to southernwood and wormwood, plants with strong bitter aromatic qualities

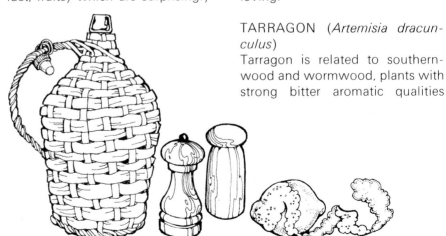

more often used in the past for their medicinal and insect-repellant properties. Tarragon, however, has a milder but distinct flavour much valued by the cook. There are two kinds of tarragon available: Russian tarragon is hardier but has little flavour and is not really worth growing; French tarragon is much better but should always be bought from a reputable source; seed will not be available. It is not, in fact, a native of France but comes from Central Asia and was probably introduced into Europe during the Moorish occupation of Southern Spain. The plant has narrow, dark green shiny leaves which may be several centimetres long, and greyish-white flower heads which should be removed to encourage leafy growth.

Tarragon needs well-drained soil, with well-rotted humus to hold moisture rather than to supply plant foods. It does best in the sun and eventually takes up quite a large space which can be filled by annuals in the first year or two. After three or four years it deteriorates in flavour unless it is divided and replanted in fresh soil. This is best done in spring as the plants are not fully hardy in all districts and a protection of strawy material, leafmould or peat is advisable in autumn.

Fresh leaves can be cut throughout the summer and cut for drying just before flowering. This, however, is difficult and not recommended, especially if you have a freezer.

Tarragon can be grown successfully in a large flower pot outdoors but is not really suitable for a window box. I remove my pot to a frame in autumn merely to give protection and I find that there is no growth to cut during the winter.

THYME (*Thymus vulgaris* — garden thyme; *T. citriodorus* — lemon thyme; *T. herba-barona* — caraway thyme)
Although we have several native thymes, the garden thyme used in cooking is a more shrubby plant and came to Britain from the Mediterranean, no doubt brought by the Romans. It has small evergreen leaves, grows about 23cm (9in) high and has spikes of clustered tiny mauve flowers.

Thyme prefers well-drained chalky soil but does surprisingly well even on heavier clays, provided it is planted in full sun. It can be started from seed but as it quickly spreads and divides easily, it is less trouble to buy a plant. It is advisable to plant in spring especially in colder districts. Little attention is needed once thyme is planted, and sprigs can be cut as required through the summer and autumn and a little even in winter from large plants, but remember that hard cutting late in the year will make the plant less hardy. Thyme for drying is best cut just before or during flowering and only one-third of the growth taken so that new shoots quickly grow again. It also freezes well.

Thyme can be propagated in several ways, either by dividing the plants in spring, by layering or by cuttings, which root easily in spring or at almost any time.

Lemon thyme has an especially pleasant scent and flavour and is pretty in its golden and golden-variegated forms. It is a more creeping plant and suitable for the rock garden where it enjoys the sharp drainage. It will turn green if it has insufficient sun or the soil is too rich. The caraway thyme (*T. herba-barona*) is also worth growing for its unusual flavour reminiscent of the herb after which it is named.

All these thymes grow well in outdoor pots or window boxes but when mixing them with other plants it is well to restrict the roots by planting them in a polythene bag (with holes for drainage) or a flower pot, so that other plants have room to grow. Pot plants can also be brought indoors or into the protection of a greenhouse or frame during the cold winter months.

As well as their medicinal and culinary virtues thymes give us charming rock plants for the garden and are described further on page 51.

Herbs from Seeds

Directions are given on most seed packets and any particular points about a herb have been dealt with separately. However, one or two general remarks may be helpful.

Hardy Annuals
Irrespective of suppliers' recommendations on times of sowing, never sow seeds during periods of inclement weather. Seeds deposited too early in cold, wet soil will merely rot, and later sowing will actually give you an earlier crop. Sowing too thickly is a common mistake and makes thinning out the seedlings a laborious task. Thin out gradually so that each plant has room to develop without touching its neighbours. Always firm the soil again carefully round the remaining plants and it is wise to water them to re-settle the soil. I often leave the plants rather closer together than suggested on the seed packets. In many garden soils the plants do not reach the proportions envisaged by seedsmen.

Seeds can be sown in rows in the vegetable garden or in patches in a herb garden or mixed border. Borage, marigolds and nasturtiums certainly look best grown in this informal way.

Half-hardy Annuals
These need more warmth to germinate and grow on successfully, before being planted out when any danger of frosts is past. It is possible to sow as early as February if a greenhouse is available. If this is not the case it is better to wait until late spring, when the

seeds can be sown in a cold frame and slowly hardened off by giving more ventilation until planting time.

Seeds may also be sown indoors at this time. Special seed propagators are available which give bottom heat, or you can make use of a shelf over a radiator or even over the back of a refrigerator which gives out heat. I sometimes use the airing cupboard but you must remember to bring out the seedlings into the light immediately they germinate. Basil, especially. needs extra warmth; that is, a temperature of about 18°C (65°F) to germinate well. All seedlings must have full light to keep them from becoming weak and drawn. They need pricking out into seed trays of compost, and are eventually planted in the garden when danger of frost is over.

All this may be daunting to the busy cook who may prefer to be content with a later crop by sowing the seed directly into the ground in late spring and early summer. Buying pot-grown basil or sweet marjoram may be well worth while if you have little time or are not blessed with green fingers.

Biennials
Biennials are hardy and may resent being transplanted, so they are usually sown where they are to grow. Angelica is usually sown in a group, caraway and parsley in rows. Parsley can also be started in seed boxes if the seedlings are pricked out carefully when they are still small.

Perennials
Seeds of some perennials are also available and this will be a considerable cash saving if you need a lot of plants. French sorrel is certainly worth starting in this way and possibly chives and Welsh onion.

Planting and Aftercare
Pot-grown plants of herbs are

generally available and recommended for planting in spring but hardy plants on light soil may well establish better in autumn and need less attention if the following spring is very dry.

Always make sure the soil is moist before removing the plant from its container. In very light soils I like to put a handful of moist peat or leafmould in the hole to give the plants a good start, and in heavier soils I also add some sharp sand. It is difficult to generalize on planting procedure and the requirements of individual plants must be studied separately; so much depends on the condition of your soil. It is worth taking special care when planting trees and shrubs. With these I usually fork some well-rotted compost into the bottom of the hole and sprinkle damp peat mixed with a handful of bonemeal round the roots before filling in (two handfuls for larger plants); this helps them to establish roots quickly in the new soil.

Once sown or planted, herbs need little attention. Many are extremely drought resistant, but remember, all plants are vulnerable to dryness at the roots during their first season.

Dividing Older Plants

After two or three years most herbaceous perennials benefit from being lifted, divided into small pieces and replanted in fresh soil. This is often best done in early spring as they start into growth, but tough plants can also be divided in autumn as suggested for individual herbs. Plants such as chives and sorrel will divide easily in the hand but vigorous growers such as lemon balm, if left undisturbed for too long, will make large clumps which will need two garden forks to separate them. Always replant the outside growth

in this case, rather than the exhausted centre. In some cases, such as horseradish, pieces of the roots are replanted with no top growth at all. When removing them from the plant it is wise to make a straight cut at the top and slanting cut at the base to ensure that they are replanted the right way up.

Taking Cuttings

The soft young growths of perennials and some shrubs can often be easily rooted. Mint and lemon balm are examples. Shoots 8 to

10cm (3 to 4in) long can be cut in summer, the lower leaves removed and a clean cut made below a leaf joint, and either rooted in water or in a special compost for cuttings. A mixture of peat and sand in equal parts is suitable but I have found proprietary soilless mixtures to be excellent both for cuttings and seed sowing. The pots of cuttings must be kept in the close atmosphere of a propagator or under a polythene bag. Geraniums are an exception and root best uncovered. Hormone rooting powder encourages quicker rooting but is not essential.

The shrubby evergreen herbs such as rosemary, lavender and sage root easiest from half-ripe cuttings. These are taken when the bases of the young shoots begin to harden from midsummer onwards. The shoots are carefully removed from the parent with a heel of the older wood attached, the lower leaves are removed and the base of each cutting is dipped in rooting hormone if desired. These cuttings can often be rooted outdoors in a semi shady place with no protection, but a jam jar, cloche or cold frame placed over them can be helpful. Sage, rosemary and lavender will root at almost any time of year, but bay is, I find, slow and difficult and a propagator with bottom heat will give more reliable results.

Elder can be propagated by hardwood cuttings; that is, shoots about 45cm (18in) long cut off in autumn after the leaves have fallen and trimmed to a leaf joint at the base. No protection is needed, just plant them firmly in well-drained soil, adding sand and peat if necessary. Lemon verbena will also root in this way. Take cuttings about 15-cm (6-in) long and keep them in warmth, as it is a much more tender plant. It can also be rooted from soft cuttings earlier in the year.

Layering
Some low-growing herbs such as thymes, marjoram and sage can be propagated by layering; that is, pegging down stems of the plant into the soil and removing them after they have rooted.

Pests and Diseases

Some herbs are remarkably resistant to pest and disease attack and others succumb from time to time, especially if conditions are not ideal. Bad drainage will cause plants to rot off, excessive dryness at the roots makes them more attractive to greenfly, and these and other insects will flourish in enclosed, very sheltered town gardens where there is little air circulation. Greenfly will attack a large number of herbs particularly chives, parsley, fennel and dill, lemon balm and sometimes mint. Blackfly favour nasturtiums and elder. A similar insect, the leaf hopper, will remove most of the green colouring matter from leaves and is prevalent in town gardens.

Great interest is being taken at present in the effect which certain plants have on others growing nearby, either making them resistant to pest and disease attack, or encouraging their growth in some way. Research is also taking place to establish which plants can best encourage beneficial insects to visit the garden. But in spite of the work of these valuable allies — ladybirds, hover flies and other insects — most people resort, from time to time, to spraying their plants with some kind of insecticide.

The most effective of these are poisonous, not only to the insects but also to animals and humans, so that great care must be taken to allow the required time to elapse before using herbs which have been sprayed with them. I prefer to use a pyrethrum-based spray which is only harmful to insects, and edible plants can be consumed as soon as needed. Also there is no risk of harming birds. Spraying should be done in the evening when there is less chance of killing bees and other pollinators, and always avoid spraying open flowers. Most herbs are resistant to diseases such as mildew, which attack a wide range of other plants, but mint is liable to rust disease especially on dry soils. Pests or diseases which attack particular herbs will be found under the cultural notes on that herb.

III
Decorative Herbs

Unfortunately, for those who presume to write on the subject, herbs do not fit neatly into groups. We can say that some are mainly useful as culinary herbs, others have particular medicinal value, or yield a dye, and some are used in cosmetics or pot-pourri. Herbs have many virtues and those which are both decorative and useful have the greatest value; particularly in the small garden where there is little room for a great number of different plants. So when selecting herbs as garden plants we can sometimes decide whether to choose the more usually grown and undoubtedly useful varieties, or to look for a more attractive form which may suit our needs just as well.

Some gardeners and flower arrangers may grow herbs purely for their beauty of flower and leaf and be unconcerned with their culinary or other uses. Herbs have a place both in formal gardens, where many can be clipped to form low hedges as in the Tudor knot gardens, and are equally at home in the informal mixed borders of shrubs and herbaceous plants where their foliage effect can be particularly valuable as background material.

Trees

Of the trees, bay has a masculine quality; tall, dark, handsome, and an asset in any garden either growing freely or clipped to a formal pyramid as in topiary. Perhaps more correctly a shrub rather than a tree, the common elder (*Sambucus nigra*) is anything but formal and makes a coarse and unattractive plant except in early spring as the leaves begin to break, and again when it is in full flower and berry. The golden kind, *aurea*, can be grown for its beautiful foliage alone and the cut-leaved green variety, *laciniata*, is perhaps even more attractive. Both these varieties will do well in semi-shade and appreciate a reasonably moist soil.

Shrubs

The culinary virtues of rosemary have already been extolled but there is no more attractive plant for the base of a sunny wall where it will grow upward, sideways and downward with graceful abandon. Miss Jessop's Upright is stiff in growth, as its name implies, but can be a useful contrast to the rounded growth of lower-growing plants such as purple sage. Rosemary in the past was used for formal hedges and even cut into topiary but I prefer to grow it naturally and merely prune out the unwanted growths after flowering. An old neglected bush can be cut really hard back in spring if necessary. The hybrid Severn Sea is an excellent variety where a lower-growing bush is required as it only reaches about 60cm (2ft) and has graceful spreading growth. The really prostrate rosemary usually listed as a rock plant is less hardy but is attractive on a sheltered sunny bank or in a tub or pot on a patio. Tuscan Blue and Benenden Blue with their beautiful bright blue flowers are also doubtfully hardy.

Lavender, another favourite garden plant, was grown in the past more for its uses than for its beauty, but Parkinson in 1629 mentions it with rosemary as a suitable plant to make a hedge or border to a knot garden. It is still planted today, most usually as a hedge, but it looks equally well planted more informally in groups in a border and associates well with shrubs and old-fashioned roses. Lavenders vary greatly in height, colour and freedom of flowering. *Lavandula spica*, the old English lavender, grows about 1m (3ft) high and flowers very freely, whereas *L. vera*, usually called Dutch lavender, has much more silvery and attractive foliage but unfortunately fewer flowers. The dwarfer forms, Hidcote, Twickel Purple and Munstead, are ideal for smaller gardens. Hidcote looks well planted in front of floribunda roses, especially the variety Lilac Charm, and also hybrid tea roses. A charming, though doubtfully hardy, rock plant is *L. stoechas*, sometimes called French lavender. The flowers are deep purple and the heads square sided with a purple tuft of leaves at the top. Lavenders must all be grown in full sun and do best in well-drained chalky soil. Instructions

for pruning and replacing by cuttings are in the A to Z section.

The artemisias are a large group of plants, many with pretty, finely cut silver leaves, mostly strongly aromatic and often with a bitter flavour making them unsuitable as culinary herbs. The exception is tarragon, (*Artemisia dracunculus*) which is probably the least attractive as a garden plant. The British native wormwood (*A. absinthium*), now naturalized in the United States, is particularly pretty and it is worth looking for the variety Lambrook Silver which grows to a graceful bush about 60cm (2ft) high. The large sprays of small brownish flowers can be cut off if you prefer an entirely silver effect. Southernwood (*A. abrotanum*), also known as lad's love and old man, has been a favourite garden plant for many centuries and the tangy sweetness of its crushed foliage made it in the past a favourite for nosegays. As one of its common names implies it symbolized the love of the lad for his lady friend. Unfortunately its fine, thread-like leaves go entirely brown in winter and the whole plant looks sad and dead. It should be cut back hard each spring and will eventually need replacing by young plants which can be easily raised from cuttings.

Cotton lavender (*Santolina chamaecyparissus*) was introduced to Britain from the Mediterranean during the 16th century and it became one of the most popular of all plants for making the low hedges which formed the patterns of Tudor knot gardens. This is not surprising as its silver-grey filigree foliage is as attractive in winter as in summer. It has a pungent but also sweet smell and is still an excellent choice today for a formal edging to a herb garden or as a low hedge. In these cases it will need to be clipped in spring and again in midsummer. Santolina can also be grown for its silver foliage effect in a mixed border, when one spring pruning

will be sufficient and even this is only necessary if the plant is becoming straggly. With less pruning you will have bright yellow button flowers, enjoyed by some, abhorred by others. There is a dwarf form especially suitable for the rock garden. *S. neapolitana* is similar in habit to the ordinary cotton lavender but has coarser growth and longer, more feathery leaves. *S. virens*, with bright green leaves, is another good dwarf shrub, especially in its variety Primrose Gem. Santolinas must have full sun to do well, and they enjoy the good drainage and alkaline soil required by so many Mediterranean and silver-foliage plants.

The Curry Plant (*Helichrysum angustifolium*) is another silver-leaved Mediterranean native which is less hardy but well worth growing in reasonably mild districts. The spiky silver foliage has a steely quality especially effective in winter. It flowers freely in summer, with golden, slightly orange-shaded button flowers and is an excellent plant – though I do find the pronounced curry smell slightly nauseating on a hot summer day. However, as mentioned in the A to Z, this quality can be an asset for flavouring.

On my well-drained chalky soil the culinary sage (*Salvia officinalis*) makes a beautiful silver-foliage plant in summer; perhaps I have a particularly good strain as most people consider it rather drear. The purple form should certainly be grown, its culinary value is equally good and medicinally it is said to be effective when used as a gargle for throat infections. It contrasts well in the garden with golden marjoram or the bright pink form of annual clary (*Salvia horminum*) usually listed as Pink Lady. I have also planted it with the hardy, pink-flowered *Geranium endressii*, and I remember a particularly pretty grouping one spring in the herb garden at Scotney Castle in Kent; the rather sombre purple was lightened by an adjoining silver-variegated thyme, with pink and blue forget-me-nots as a foreground and the pale yellow tulip Sweet Harmony behind. *S. officinalis tricolor*, with leaves of pink, white and green, is exceptionally pretty and the yellow-variegated Icterina is another effective foliage plant. This I like to grow with pale yellow flowers such as petunia Brass Band or others of yellow, gold or orange shades.

Rue, especially in its form Jackman's Blue, is perhaps the most effective of all herbs as a foliage plant. Gerard in his Herbal describes it thus: 'the leaves hereof consist of divers parts, and be divided into wings, about which are certaine little ones, of an odd number, something broad, more long than round, smooth and somewhat fat, of a grey colour or greenish blew'. It is all these qualities of shape, texture and colour which can be used with such advantage in association with other plants. It can be grown as a foreground to the beautiful blue flax, *Linum perenne*, just one of many suitable neighbours. The variety *variegata* has young leaves partially coloured deep cream or white.

Hyssop is less attractive as a foliage plant but is quite a pretty low growing shrub, especially in the form with bright blue flowers. It can be grown on a sunny bank and I have seen it prettily associated in the Queen's Garden at Kew with our wild heartsease, *Viola tricolor*.

Herbaceous Perennials

Apart from elder, all the decorative trees and shrubs mentioned must have full sun to do well; perennials on the other hand, several of which are native to Britain, are generally less sun loving and several do better in a shaded, moist soil. Quite apart from its culinary value I would certainly grow angelica, either as a single plant, where space is limited, or as an imposing group. Sweet Cicely with its delicate ferny foliage and lacy white flower heads does well in part shade and salad burnet will carpet the ground in similar conditions or in full sun. Sweet woodruff is a charming ground-cover plant preferring moist soil and some shade.

There is no denying that mints have a strong tendency to overrun their allotted space and penetrate amongst other plants, but I find the more decorative-leaved varieties are less invasive and well worth growing. Eau de Cologne mint has attractive deep purple young growth, ginger mint has leaves splashed with gold and makes attractive ground cover, easily pulled out if it strays too far. There is no such problem with the variegated apple mint (*Mentha rotundifolia variegata*) which should be grown in every garden. Its only similarity to the invasive culinary apple mint is the hairy, felted texture of the leaf. These leaves are narrower and longer and prettily marked with white and soft green. I find it does best in semi-shade for it wilts quickly if the soil becomes too dry. This also happens when it is cut and it must be quickly put into water. Bearing this in mind it makes an excellent culinary mint.

Fennel foliage makes an attractive background to other plants and black fennel is particularly effective. The leaves are, in fact, a dark bronze colour and contrast well with yellow and orange flowers as in the cottage garden at Sissinghurst Castle in Kent.

Lemon balm has both a golden-variegated form and also one with entirely gold leaves. Unfortunately they are both listed as *Melissa officinalis aurea* so check the description in your nursery catalogue. The pure gold form has, I find, less lemon scent but I consider it the more attractive plant of the two.

The golden forms of marjoram make an attractive display in the garden. They have some culinary value and are among the best lower-growing golden foliage plants. It prefers sun but resents too dry a soil; in ideal conditions it can grow 60cm (2ft) high and contrasts well with annual clary (*Salvia horminum*) in its purple form, Blue Beard, or with purple sage and other darker-leaved plants.

So far we have considered herbs mainly for their foliage value in the garden. Tansy (*Tanecetum vulgare*), a British native plant, has attractive bright green cut leaves and clusters of bright yellow button flowers on stems up to 1m (3ft) high. The variety *crispum* has more cut and parsley-like leaves. Tansy spreads rapidly but can be kept under control by dividing and replanting as necessary.

We grow bergamot in our gardens and herb gardens more often for the brilliant colour of its flowers than to make the famous Oswego tea. Most often seen is *Monarda didyma* Cambridge Scarlet, a brilliant but not harsh red enhanced by the ring of bracts below the flower head which are tinged with purple. Croftway Pink is a good rose-coloured variety, and Prairie Night a rich purple. The latter is the result of a cross with *M. fistulosa* which suggests it may be a good variety to grow if you have not the moist conditions which most Bergamots prefer.

Comfrey (*Symphytum officinale*) is best known for its remarkable medicinal qualities and is particularly valuable as a forage crop for animals. It was at one time grown in large quantities for feeding at Whipsnade Zoo and was by far the favourite delicacy of the hippopotamus! As a decorative garden plant it is coarse in growth but the arching clusters of cream or purple flowers are attractive. *S.*

caucasicum is dwarf — about 60cm (2ft) high — and has brilliant blue flowers in spring. *S. grandiflorum* has red-tipped buds and creamy yellow flowers and spreads quickly even under trees, making a useful weed-smothering ground cover, only about (1ft) high. There is also an attractive form with variegated leaves. These leaves, however, easily revert to plain green and this may explain why the plant is difficult to obtain. All comfreys enjoy some shade or at least a reasonably moist soil and the taller varieties look well growing in natural surroundings bordering a large pool, though they can be invasive and difficult to remove once established.

There are, rather confusingly, two plants with the common name of clary (the name originating from 'clear-eyes' and indicating its medicinal use in the past for bathing and soothing the eyes and re-

Lavender makes a good companion for many plants. Here it looks well in a bed of roses

moving foreign bodies). *Salvia sclarea* and its variety *turkestanica* are short-lived perennial or biennial plants and the last named is most easily obtainable from nurseries. Clary was one of the first herbs introduced to America from Europe. Considered by some to be coarse in growth, I find them strikingly beautiful plants. They grow about 1m (3ft) high and carry large sprays of flowers, which are mauve or white, accompanied by pink bracts (coloured leaves) which remain and look attractive after the flowers have faded. Clary is a good plant to blend with stronger shades of pink, mauve, purple and blue.

Annuals

Although borage (*Borago officinalis*) is strictly an annual or biennial plant, once established it will seed itself and you will have little fear of losing it. The charming clear blue flowers with their dark cone of stamens were often illustrated in the flowery borders of old manuscripts and in Tudor and Stuart needlework. Unfortunately, the plants grow almost too quickly with untidy straggling stems, so that these and the dead flowers must be cut off from time to time. Grown amongst shrub roses it can be an informal ground cover and the rose stems will support the borage. When sowing seeds in spring and summer just press two or three about 2·5cm (1in) into the soil about 60cm (2ft) apart where you want your plants to grow. As they develop, thin the groups to leave single plants. If you do not have room to grow the ordinary borage you might like to try *B. laxiflora*, a miniature spreading plant only 23cm (9in) high. This species is a perennial and listed by alpine specialist nurseries.

Even the least experienced gardener can usually recognize the marigold, but most people are surprised to see it growing among collections of herbs. The petals of pot marigold (*Calendula officinalis*) were used a great deal in the past for flavouring, for adding colour both to sweet and savoury dishes and for garnishing the flowery salads of earlier times. In the 18th century the petals were used as a substitute for the more expensive saffron in colouring cheeses and butter. The pot marigold must not be confused with the French or African marigold — it will be found in seed catalogues usually under its Latin name *Calendula*. You may prefer to grow the ordinary species or one of the modern strains such as Art Shades, with apricot, orange and cream flowers, or for a window box or front of a border the new dwarfer varieties Baby Gold and Baby Orange.

The nasturtium has already been described fully as a culinary herb, but it has many shades of yellow and orange and also red and crimson which will add colour to the garden. There is a new strain called Alaska with variegated leaves of cream and green. This can be an effective foliage plant, flowers well and is seemingly less attractive to blackfly.

One of my favourite annuals is the annual clary, *Salvia horminum*. The flowers are hardly noticeable but the large leafy bracts are brilliantly coloured purple, pink or white. You can buy mixed packets or purple or pink separately, whichever fits best into your colour scheme. Several associations with foliage have already been suggested. It does not do well in hot dry weather but in the average English summer it will continue to flower well into the autumn and is invaluable for cutting for arrangements. Another flower arranger's 'herb' is the orach or mountain spinach which has been grown as a vegetable since Roman times, but is usually chosen today in its coloured-leaved forms: *Atriplex hortensis cupreata* or *A. hortensis rubra*. Both have dark red leaves and purple stems and seed heads and grow quickly to

(rooted offsets) for one square metre or one square yard to obtain adequate cover.

Thyme lawns can be started by sowing your own seeds or buying plants — again you need an open sunny position and light, quickly draining soil. Mints are a better choice for moist, shady areas and the crushed leaves of pennyroyal have a delicious scent and the mauve flower spikes are pretty. There is a prostrate form particularly suited to carpeting and it spreads rapidly. *Mentha requienii* which only reaches 5cm (2in), has tiny leaves and flowers and a refreshing peppermint scent. It is less tough and not as vigorous but is well worth growing.

Grow any or all of these decorative plants either to add colour, beauty and scent to your collection of culinary herbs or anywhere where they will grow well and be a part of your whole garden picture.

Herbs for Flower Arrangements

Unless they are also cooks and gardeners, flower arrangers should never be allowed alone amongst the herbs or for that matter in any other part of the garden! Bearing this in mind there are a number of herbs which will actually benefit from having their flowers cut.

Cutting off the large greenish flower heads of angelica will prolong the life of the plant, but supposing you want to crystallize the stems? The answer of course is to grow enough for both if you have the room. The green flowers of lovage could again be effective in large arrangements and here the cooks will fortunately be mainly concerned with the leaves, the same applies to the pretty flowers of marjoram and chives. Bergamot will supply bright flower heads for cutting if you are prepared to sacrifice the garden effect, catmint on the other hand usually produces

1·25m (4ft) high. I have seen them effectively contrasted with the white Californian poppy, *Romneya coulteri*, at Powis Castle on the Welsh border. Another purple-leaved annual is the form of basil called Dark Opal which is hardier than its culinary relation and can be sown directly into the ground in spring. It is aromatic but not recommended for flavouring.

Our Lady's milk thistle (*Silybum marianum*) is seldom grown but its white-veined, dark green, thistle-like leaves give striking foliage effect.

Rock Plants

There are a number of low-growing and creeping herbs which are admirably suited to growing as rock plants. You can mix culinary and decorative herbs on a sunny bank with perhaps a few stones to hold back the soil, especially until the plants are established. Here is a home for winter savory

(so generous with its tiny flowers in late summer and autumn), hyssop, marjorams, thymes and chamomile.

Garden thyme itself is pretty in flower and leaf but I am especially fond of the silver-variegated kind Silver Posie. With it I grow dwarf alpine pinks and a carpet of *Thymus serpyllum*, our wild creeping thyme, on a slightly sloping bed. These plants are also ideal to grow in specially made gaps in paving or at the sides of paths. The golden-variegated lemon thyme is especially pretty in spring and there is also an entirely golden form. Creeping herbs are often suggested for lawns and paths but can be rather expensive on anything but the smallest scale, and annoyingly slow to establish and difficult to weed. I prefer to plant chamomile in pockets among paving, but if you wish to make a lawn it is best to buy the non-flowering variety Treneague. You must have well-drained and prepared soil which is free of perennial weeds and in full sun. You will need about 80 plantlets so many graceful sprays of tiny mauve flowers that you can happily cut, for they will come again. The flower spikes of mint are particularly attractive to use in late summer.

An old medicinal herb and one of my favourite plants both in the garden and for arranging is *Alchemilla mollis*, or lady's mantle. The sprays of tiny acid-yellow flowers last well and the beautifully scalloped leaves are invaluable. Tansy gives you long-lasting yellow button flowers which can be dried for winter arrangements, the bright green cut leaves are also useful. Annuals will give the greatest number of flowers for cutting from midsummer onwards; among them marigolds and nasturtiums in a wide range of colours from yellow through orange to red, but most valuable of all, perhaps, is the annual clary with its tall and very striking purple, pink or white bracts which last so well in water.

Fortunately some of the valuable foliage plants are not required by the cook. Many people grow the cardoon, *Cynara cardunculus*, (related to the globe artichoke) for its bold garden effect and large, beautifully shaped grey leaves. Curry plant, southernwood, wormwood (Lambrook Silver) and cotton lavender will give you silver-grey foliage, though the latter is rather bunchy in growth and the

species *neapolitana* is more graceful. Use purple sage, the gold-variegated Icterina, and the feathery leaves of fennel (both green and bronze) when they can be spared. Rue is ideal for flower arrangement, especially in its variety Jackman's Blue which is seldom required by the cook, and the leaves last extremely well when cut. If allowed to flower it gives attractive seed pods for drying. Another foliage 'must' for arrangers is the annual red-leaved Orach, (*Atriplex hortensis cupreata*) already described as a decorative garden plant especially attractive when the seed heads are forming. If you can spare them the leaves and seed heads of angelica and lovage are good to use in large arrangements, as are those of the delicate fern-like sweet Cicely. The latter wilts easily and should be laid in cool or warm water for a few hours before arranging.

Below left: *The golden variegated form of lemon balm* (Melissa officinalis aurea)

Below right: *Variegated mint* (Mentha rotundifolia variegata)

53

IV
Herbal Preparations

Herb Teas

We are not qualified to write on the medicinal use of herbs as cures for illness, but can recommend using them for tisanes or herb teas. Many plants both wild and cultivated can be used for these infusions. A favourite in France is made with lime flowers. We have made a short list of cultivated herbs included in the A to Z which we consider most valuable or pleasant to drink as an occasional mild tonic, sedative or to aid digestion. The tisane is made in the same way as ordinary tea, that is one teaspoon of dried herbs for each cup and one for the pot. When using fresh herbs you will need as much as three times this amount, and it helps to break up the leaves a little in most cases or crush them slightly. Warm the pot (which should not be made of metal) as usual, and pour boiling water on to the leaves. Allow the pot to stand for 5 to 10 minutes. Be sure to replace the lid — these infusions must be covered or much of their value will be lost in steam. Pour the tea into cups in the normal manner — omitting the milk of course!

When making a tea from seeds you will have to make a decoction. The seeds will need crushing well, preferably with a pestle and mortar. Add them to boiling water (in an enamel pan) and simmer them for about 10 minutes before straining. You will need about 2 teaspoons of seed to one pint of water.

Herbs can be both stimulating and soothing at the same time. The following are aids to digestion and relaxation: angelica, anise (seeds), bergamot, caraway (seeds), chamomile (flowers), cumin (seeds), dill (seeds), elder (usually flowers but leaves may also be used in spring), fennel (leaves or seeds), lemon balm, lemon geranium, lemon verbena, lovage (savoury flavour to which salt may be added), marigold (petals), marjoram, mints (especially peppermint), thyme and woodruff (best used dried). Sweet Cicely can also be used (leaves or seeds) but the main value of this herb is in flavouring and reducing acidity in cooked fruits.

Herbs having a tonic and sometimes stimulating effect are: angelica, borage, comfrey, lemon balm, rosemary, sage, woodruff and, particularly on the liver and kidneys, juniper berries. If, however, you have a chronic illness you must seek the advice of your doctor.

For colds, elder flower, marjoram and sage are recommended, and the latter is also good for gargling if you have a sore throat. (Use purple sage if possible.) Parsley tea is an especially valuable source of vitamin C and is said to be good for rheumatism. The teas may be flavoured if you wish — honey blends well as a sweetener, and a slice of lemon enhances some teas.

Devotees of Beatrix Potter may remember that after Peter Rabbit had been overeating in Mr McGregor's garden, his mother put him to bed with chamomile tea while Flopsy, Mopsy and Cottontail had bread and milk and blackberries!

Pot-pourri

The making of pot-pourri can be a fascinating hobby; whole books have been written on the subject and these make fascinating reading. Recipes go back to Elizabethan times and some of the suggested ingredients are now unobtainable or expensive to buy. Once you understand the main principles of pot-pourri making, and what each constituent contributes to the final result, you can make up your own recipes according to the flowers and herbs which you have available to use. Most people prefer to make a dry pot-pourri rather than a moist one preserved in salt. The latter holds the scent longer but does not look attractive.

To form the bulk of your material you need scented flowers or petals, and here is the first snag. It is no good waiting until the petals are ready to fall. Flowers must be cut in their prime, and lavender when only the first flowers are opening. This can be a considerable sacrifice in a small garden and I certainly would find it hard to cut tiny rose buds as sometimes recommended. These two, lavender

and roses, do retain their scent exceptionally well when dried. Use any strongly scented roses, particularly the old varieties such as the apothecary's rose (*R. gallica officinalis*), the Provence rose (*R. centifolia*), and the damask rose (*R. damascena*), or modern hybrid teas such as Fragrant Cloud, Ena Harkness and Silver Lining. Other flowers to use are pinks and carnations, jasmine, violets, philadephus (mock orange), honeysuckle, sweet Cicely, stocks, mignonette and heliotrope. Use the flowers and leaves of thyme, marjoram, rosemary and hyssop.

Herbs and plants with aromatic leaves make an important contribution, particularly lemon verbena and the various scented-leaved geraniums (really pelargoniums) such as the rose-scented geranium and the lemon-scented *Pelargonium crispum*. The mints (pineapple and eau de Cologne), lemon thyme, angelica, bergamot, sweet woodruff, southernwood and sweet briar are also very useful. Some flowers are used more for their colourful effect than for their scent; for example, borage flowers, marigold petals, and the flowers of chamomile, costmary and bergamot.

Flowers and leaves for pot-pourri are dried in the same way as herbs for cooking. Cut them when they are dry after the morning dew has dispersed, and keep them on racks or trays in a warm, dark, airy place. Large flowers such as roses must have their petals removed to dry singly (unless you are just drying the buds). Dried leaves are usually rubbed through a sieve before using.

The next constituent of most pot-pourri is a fixative, which helps to retain the essential oils which give the mixture its ·fragrance. Dried orris root can be obtained, or you can grow the plant (*Iris germanica florentina*) and dry the roots yourself. A substitute can be lemon or orange peel carefully pared off without

pith, and minced or ground finely after drying in a cool oven.

Essential oils are helpful if your pot-pourri is not already strongly scented. These can be obtained from herbalists, and comprise such substances as rose geranium or lavender oil, or a mixture especially blended for making the pot-pourri, or reviving its fragrance at a later date. Many people like to add spices such as cinnamon, nutmeg, cloves or powdered ginger to pot-pourri.

When your flowers and leaves are dry (after about ten days), mix them with all the other ingredients and store the pot-pourri in a sealed container in the dark for about six weeks, stirring or shaking it daily. It can then be transferred to other containers such as china bowls, but always keep these covered when the mixture is not in use (this conserves the scent).

Recipe for pot-pourri (Quantities after drying)
4 cups rose petals
2 cups lavender flowers
1 cup other scented flowers
1 cup scented leaves
$\frac{1}{3}$ cup orris root powder
2 tablespoons mixed spices
few drops of essential oils or pot-pourri reviver

Herb Sachets and Pillows

Strongly scented herbs such as lavender and lemon verbena are especially good for using alone, or combined, in sachets or sweet bags to place among clothes in drawers, and to hang in cupboards or about the room. The material must be open enough to allow the scent, but not the ingredients, to penetrate outwards. A flat sachet can be quilted by machine to keep the contents evenly spread. A charming lavender 'basket' can be made by taking about 11 spikes of freshly cut

Nasturtium (Tropaeolum majus)

Parsley (Petroselinum crispum) *variety Bravour*

Lavender baskets can easily be made by tying several flower spikes together just below the flower heads, bending the stalks back and threading coloured ribbon in between them to give a basketwork effect. Tie the ends of the ribbon round the stems to make a bow or loop

Apart from being made into baskets, the flower spikes of lavender can also be arranged as fans. Tie the heads into a muslin bag and thread ribbon through the stems, pulling them into the shape of a fan

Herbs for Beauty and the Bath

It is possible now to buy many herbal cosmetics, soaps and bath oils, and many people find their subtle fragrance particularly acceptable. They are refreshing and beneficial to the skin. Making some of these beauty aids is not a practical proposition for anybody but the single-minded devotee. Elder Flower Water, as obtained from herbalists, is a distilled essence and is excellent as a night and morning cleanser, especially for dry skins. You can make your own water from fresh or dried flowers in the same way as a tisane, but do not make too much at once as it will only keep for a few days.

lavender on long stalks. Tie them together tightly below the heads and then turn back the stalks so that the heads lie between them. Weave narrow ribbon in and out between the stalks in a basket work pattern starting nearest the heads and finishing with a bow lower down on the stalks. If you have enough dried material to spare, stuff small pillows. Placed under the normal pillow they give scented, restful nights to yourself or your guests. Angelica, southern-

wood and woodruff are good for this, along with the wild lady's bedstraw (*Galium verum*), and lemon verbena, rosemary leaves and dried pine needles. Make up the mixture as for pot-pourri, using a fixative and essential oils if you wish. Dried hops can be used to fill normal-sized pillows recommended for insomnia and asthma sufferers. Your cat would enjoy a small pillow filled with dried cat-mint, or you can use it to stuff a toy mouse.

If you can spare enough rosemary it makes an excellent hair rinse. 25g (1oz) of dried or fresh leaves (and flowers if you wish) are simmered in about 570ml (1 pint) of water for ten minutes. Strain to remove the leaves and add the solution to the water for your final rinse. Your hair will be soft, shining and fragrant. Rosemary is the best herb to use if you have dark hair, but blondes should use chamomile. Fresh or dried herbs make refreshing and often deliciously scented baths, but you do need rather a lot of material to make a really scented bath. Allow at least 25g (1oz) of dried herbs and 55g (2 oz) of fresh, to 570ml (1 pint) of boiling water and add this (strained) to the bath water. The soft leaves of lemon balm, angelica, lovage, marjoram and elder flowers can be infused as if making a tisane. The harder leaves of thyme, rosemary and bay should be simmered for about 10 minutes before straining and adding to the bath. These are only suggestions; try others and blend them if you wish. If you can only spare a few sprigs tie them in a muslin bag to the bath tap so that the hot water runs through them.

Sachets can be made in many shapes and with a variety of materials. a) A lavender or pot-pourri bag is one of the easiest to make. A square or circle of material is drawn together with a ribbon around a handful of the scented mixture. b) Offcuts from net curtains can be sewn together to sandwich some colourful pot-pourri. Cut around the edges with pinking shears to finish off. c) A heart-shaped sachet, edged with lace, can be decorated with a sprig of lavender or other dried flowers. d) A quilted sachet. After stuffing, the sachet is sewn together with criss-cross lines so that the contents are held in place. e) A circular sachet decorated with lace

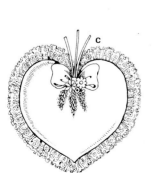

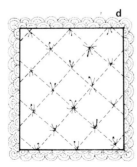

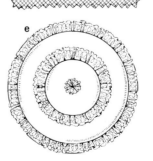

V
Harvesting and Storing Herbs

A good cook uses fresh herbs whenever they are available, but as winter approaches the choice and quantity for cutting becomes increasingly limited. The good gardener will be able to supply at least some fresh herbs throughout the winter but these can be supplemented by a store of dried herbs harvested in the bountiful summer months.

Drying

If you have made one or two half-hearted and unsuccessful attempts at drying herbs it is easy to become disillusioned and buy from the stores.

What has gone wrong? The following important points may be helpful.

1. Just before flowering many herbs have increased amounts of volatile oils which give them their flavour; so this is often the best time to cut them.

2. Volatile oils are lost in hot sunshine so cutting should take place in the early morning after the dew has dried.

3. Cut the stems with sharp scissors or secateurs and lay them carefully on clean paper in a flat basket so that the leaves are not damaged.

4. Rinse with tepid water if necessary and dry at once. Absorbent paper kitchen towels are ideal for this.

5. Herbs must be dried in the dark, not in sunshine as many people suppose.

6. To keep colour and flavour, quick drying and a temperature which is not too high are both important. Aim for a temperature of between 27 and 38°C (80 to 100°F).

7. There must be a free circulation of air to remove the humidity caused by moisture being released from the leaves.

Numbers 5, 6 and 7 can be achieved in various ways. Larger-leaved herbs such as sage can be hung in small loose bunches. The hanger rail of an unused clothes cupboard is ideal for this but the doors must be left open. If practicable a cool oven can be used for drying small quantities of herbs. Aga type cookers are useful for this. Particularly recommended for most herbs are pieces of netting attached to a wooden framework. Wooden boxes, normally called

Golden-variegated sage (Salvia officinalis
Icterina) and the purple-leaved variety

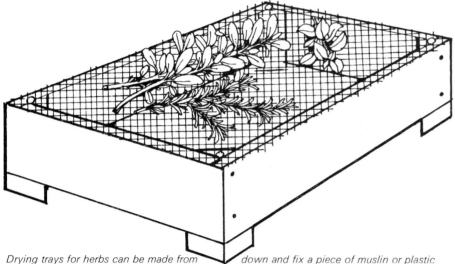

Drying trays for herbs can be made from old tomato boxes or 'Dutch trays'. Knock out the wooden slats or hardboard which forms the bottom, turn the tray upside down and fix a piece of muslin or plastic netting into place with four drawing pins. The herbs will dry well with a good circulation of air around them

tomato boxes or Dutch trays, can be obtained from greengrocers. Turn each box upside down, remove the wooden base and replace it with nylon netting or muslin. You will then have a tray supported on four 'feet' which allows air to circulate freely. Then find your warm dark place such as a loft or attic. The herbs are ready to store when the leaves are brittle and crumble easily; they should not be powdery.

Store in air-tight containers. If these are made of glass they must be kept in a cupboard to exclude light. Never store in paper or polythene bags. Properly dried herbs should retain their flavour for at least a year but will not keep indefinitely.

Seed heads are cut for drying just before they are fully ripe or the seeds will drop as you gather them. They can be hung in bunches in muslin bags or where they can drop onto paper below.

Flowers and petals for pot-pourri are dried in the same way as leaves. As all herbs and flowers are not ready for drying at the same time, the amount of space required is less than you might imagine.

Freezing

If you have a freezer, this is an excellent way to store fresh herbs as they retain their natural colour as well as flavour.

Chervil and parsley (which are not rewarding to dry) freeze very successfully, but the tougher leaves of rosemary, bay and the curry plant are better dried. You will find recommendations for storing herbs in the A to Z section.

The rules for harvesting herbs for freezing are the same as for gathering them for drying.

It is not necessary to blanch herbs before freezing, just rinse them in cold water, dry them carefully between sheets of absorbent paper and seal the sprigs in small polythene bags. Label the bags carefully and place them together in a box to protect them.

The sprays go limp when defrosted, so they cannot be used for garnishing in the same way as fresh herbs, but the frozen leaves crumble very easily so do not need to be defrosted and chopped. As an approximate guide, 55g (2oz) frozen whole leaves will give you about 1 tablespoon of chopped herbs.

It is a good idea to have some bags containing sprays of two or three different herbs combined to suit your particular taste. These can later be crumbled or used whole as bouquet garni. Tie a string round the stalk end of the faggot, long enough to tie the other end on the handle of the saucepan, or extract them at the end of cooking with the kitchen tongs.

To save space in your freezer, you can chop the herbs before freezing and seal them in conveniently small containers. Label them carefully and put them where they can be easily found when you want them.

Some people suggest freezing chopped herbs in ice cubes, but you may not always feel you want your sauce or soup cooled at the last minute with melting ice. It is easier to sprinkle the chopped frozen herbs directly on to the food to be garnished or flavoured. On the other hand, whole mint leaves frozen in ice cubes make an attractive garnish to float in wine or fruit cups.

VI
A-Z of Herbs

This section contains at-a-glance details of the cultivation, harvesting, propagation and uses of all the major garden herbs which are grown for either their culinary value or their decorative appearance. More detailed information will be found under the appropriate headings in Chapters II and III

ANGELICA

(Angelica archangelica)

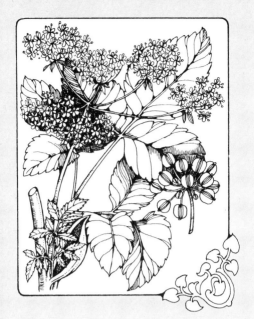

Description: Perennial with large divided leaves and flowering stems up to 2·5m (8ft) in summer.

Where to grow: Good, well-drained moist soil, preferably in shade.

Propagation: Sow newly ripe seeds where required to grow in late summer. Divide in spring.

Planting time: Spring.

Available fresh: Leaves and leaf stems in spring and summer.

Harvesting for storage: Cut flower stems for crystallizing in late spring. Leaves best cut for drying and freezing early summer. Cut seed heads when ripe in late summer.

Special tip: Sow fresh seed only.

Flavour: Seeds and leaves have delicate muscatel flavour. Young leaves have strong subtle flavour.

Culinary uses: Crystallize young stems to decorate cakes, desserts; add chopped to puddings, cakes, cream cheese. Fresh leaves give fragrance to fruit compotes, preserves, cold fruit and wine drinks.

Other uses: Herbal tea; herb bath; dried leaves for herb pillows and pot-pourri. Flowers enjoyed by bees. Decorative garden plant.

ANISE

(Pimpinella anisum)

Description: Half-hardy annual with feathery leaves and clusters of small white flowers in mid-summer. Reaches height of 45cm (18in).

Where to grow: Light, well-drained soil in full sun.

Propagation: Seed sown where required to grow.

Sowing time: Late spring.

Available fresh: Leaves can be cut all summer.

Harvesting for storage: Cut stems to harvest seed just before fully ripe in late summer.

Special tip: Seed will only ripen in long hot summer so bought supply will be more reliable.

Flavour: Pungent, similar to caraway.

Culinary uses: Add crushed seeds to soups, fish dishes, cold desserts, cakes, biscuits. Scatter finely chopped fresh leaves on cooked vegetables and salads.

Other uses: Aniseed tea. A pretty garden annual.

BASIL

(Ocimum basilicum)

Description: Bushy half-hardy annual with glossy green leaves. Small white flowers mid- to late summer. Height, 45 cm. (18in).

Where to grow: Well-drained soil, sheltered sunny position.

Propagation: Seed best sown in greenhouse or frame in spring.

Planting time: Early summer.

Available fresh: Leaves in summer.

Harvesting for storage: Cut leaves for drying just before plant flowers (or in late summer). Flavour retained better by freezing.

Special tips: Pinch out shoot tips to prevent flowering. Bush basil is easier to grow.

Flavour: Fresh leaves have sweet spicy flavour; dried are more peppery but gradually lose aroma.

Culinary uses: Especially good with tomato, garlic and wine dishes, Mediterranean vegetables and salads. Add to soups, sauces, marinades, basting sauces, fish, meat, poultry, game, sausages, egg, cheese and pasta dishes. Use to flavour Basil Vinegar and Wine.

Other uses: Variety Dark Opal has ornamental purple leaves.

BAY
(*Laurus nobilis*)

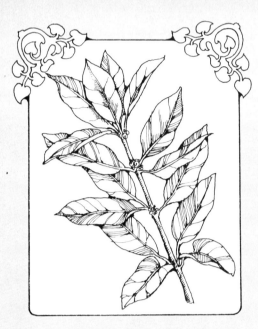

Description: A bushy tree with dark, evergreen leaves. Up to 18m (60ft) high but container-grown plants can be kept below 2m (6ft).
Where to grow: Ordinary garden soil or in tubs. Sunny, sheltered position.
Propagation: Heel cuttings, summer.
Planting time: Spring.
Available fresh: All year.
Harvesting for storage: Cut leaves for drying in summer.
Special tip: Guard from cold winds and hard frost in winter.

Flavour: Fresh leaves have strong aromatic flavour. One per dish is usually sufficient, infused during cooking then withdrawn. Dried leaves gradually diminish in flavour.
Culinary uses: Essential ingredient in bouquet garni. Infuse leaves in marinades, basting sauces, stocks, soups, sauces (sweet and savoury), with fish, meat, poultry, game, vegetable dishes. Use fresh leaves to garnish pâtés, kebabs, stuffed tomatoes.
Other uses: Herb bath. Decorative formal evergreen for tubs.

BERGAMOT
(*Monarda didyma*)

Description: Perennial. Bright red flowers early to late summer. Height about 60–100cm (2–3ft).
Where to grow: Good moist soil, sun or part shade.
Propagation: Division of clumps.
Planting time: Spring.
Available fresh: Leaves spring to autumn. Flowers mid- to late summer.
Harvesting for storage: Cut leaves for drying as flowering begins. Dry flowers as available.
Special tip: Divide and replant every two or three years.

Flavour: Leaves are lemon scented, flowers are perfumed.
Culinary uses: Chopped leaves may be used for salads, whole leaves to flavour wine cups. Flowers can be used to garnish savoury and sweet dishes. 'Berga-mottes de Lorraine' are scented, boiled sweets sold in France.
Other uses: Herbal tea; dried leaves and flowers for pot-pourri. Very decorative border plant. Good for bees.

BORAGE
(*Borago officinalis*)

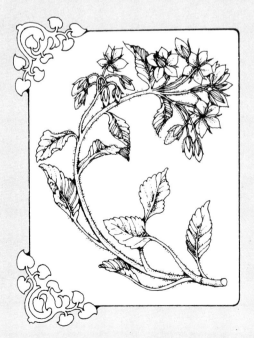

Description: Hardy annual or bi-ennial with large rough leaves and usually clear blue flowers. Height about 60cm (2ft).
Where to grow: Well-drained soil, sunny position.
Propagation: Seeds sown where required to grow.
Sowing time: Spring to midsummer.
Available fresh: Young leaves and flowers in summer.
Harvesting for storage: Drying leaves difficult, but they freeze well. Flowers can be dried.
Special tip: Plants are rather coarse and spreading so allow some space.
Flavour: Fresh cucumber.
Culinary uses: Flowers and young leaves are edible, older leaves too bristly. Add finely chopped leaves to salads, yogurt, cream cheese. Fry whole leaves in sweet batter. Use flowers and young leaves to garnish and flavour wine cups, Pimms No. 1 and apple juice.
Other uses: Herbal tea from fresh or dried leaves and flowers; dried flowers for colour in pot-pourri. Decorative garden plant. Good for bees.

CARAWAY
(Carum carvi)

Description: Biennial or perennial with leaves like parsley and roots like parsnip. Clusters of small white flowers, early to midsummer, on stems 30–60cm (1–2ft) high.
Where to grow: Well-drained soil and sunny position.
Propagation: Seeds sown where required to grow.
Sowing time: Late spring.
Available fresh: Leaves in summer, roots in winter.
Harvesting for storage: Cut stems of ripe seed in midsummer one year after sowing.

Special tip: Do not transplant.
Flavour: Seeds have strong aromatic flavour; leaves are milder.
Culinary uses: Seeds are used in cream cheese, goulash, red and green cabbage, cakes, biscuits, bread. Use fresh leaves in marinades and salads. Roots can be boiled as vegetable.
Other uses: Herbal tea.

CHAMOMILE
(Anthemis nobilis)

Description: Creeping perennial with finely cut fragrant leaves. Small, white, daisy-like flowers, early to midsummer, on stalks about 15cm (6in) high.
Where to grow: Good light soil, sunny position.
Propagation: Seed sown where required to grow, but preferably division, both in spring.
Planting time: Spring.
Available fresh: Flowers as they fully open.
Harvesting for storage: Drying of flowers recommended. Successive pickings as they are ready.
Special tip: For a chamomile lawn, plant non-flowering variety.
Flavour: Distinctive, strong fragrance, not suitable for cooking.
Other uses: Herbal tea; hair rinse, especially for blondes; dried flowers for pot-pourri.

CHERVIL
(Anthriscus cerefolium)

Description: Annual with delicate, lacy, green leaves and clusters of tiny white flowers in summer. Height, 45cm (18in).
Where to grow: Well-drained soil. Half shade in summer; sunny position for winter crop.
Propagation: Seeds sown where required to grow.
Sowing time: Spring and summer.
Available fresh: Leaves six to eight weeks after sowing.
Harvesting for storage: Unsuitable for drying. Freezes well.
Special tips: Soil must always be moist. Cut leaves regularly and remove flower heads.
Flavour: Delicate aniseed flavour, volatile, so add towards the end of cooking.
Culinary uses: Traditional ingredient of 'fines herbes' mixture for omelettes. Add chopped leaves to sauces (hot and cold), soups, egg dishes, cream cheese, fish, shellfish, meat, poultry, game, vegetables, salads, salad dressings, savoury butter. Alternative to parsley as garnish.
Other uses: None.

CHIVES
(Allium schoenoprasum)

Description: Perennial with tufts of long, thin, hollow leaves and mauve flowers. Height about 18cm (7in).

Where to grow: Preferably rich soil and sunny position.

Propagation: Division of clumps. Can also be grown from seed sown in spring where required to grow.

Planting time: Usually spring to autumn.

Available fresh: Early to late summer.

Harvesting for storage: Not very suitable for drying. Freezes well.

Special tips: Cut frequently to 5cm (2in) above ground to encourage new growth. Cut off flower heads if not required.

Flavour: Delicate onion flavour.

Culinary uses: Finely snipped leaves make flavoursome garnish on soups, salads, vegetables, fish, meat, poultry. Use instead of coarser flavoured onion in salad dressings, sauces, delicately flavoured dishes of fish, shellfish, white meat. Flowers make attractive garnish for salads.

Other uses: Good edging plant.

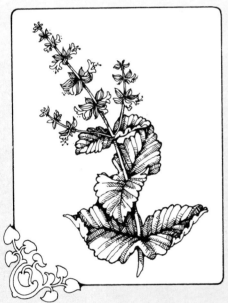

CLARY
(Salvia sclarea)

Description: Perennial but usually acts as biennial. Large, tough, heart-shaped leaves. Spikes of mauve-pink flowers mid- to late summer. Height, 1m (3ft).

Where to grow: Well-drained soil, sunny position.

Propagation: Seed sown in spring where required to grow.

Planting time: Spring or autumn.

Available fresh: Young leaves in summer.

Harvesting for storage: Leaves retain flavour well when dried or frozen.

Special tip: Fresh leaves are available in winter if protected.

Flavour: Leaves have sharpish, unusual flavour, very aromatic. Use with discretion.

Culinary uses: Can be used as ordinary sage; fry in sweet batter; add to wine cups and fruit drinks.

Other uses: A very decorative plant for the border or herb garden. Do not confuse with *Salvia horminum*, also called clary. This is an annual only 45cm (18in) high with purple, pink or white bracts.

COMFREY
(Symphytum officinale)

Description: Perennial. Large, tapering, bristly leaves. Curled heads of tube-like flowers, usually white, pink or purple, from early summer to autumn. Height, 60–100cm (2–3ft).

Where to grow: Preferably damp soil in sun or part shade.

Propagation: Division or seed sown where required to grow, both in spring.

Planting time: Spring or autumn.

Available fresh: Leaves in spring, summer and autumn.

Harvesting for storage: Drying leaves is particularly difficult.

Special tips: A coarse rather invasive plant. Ideal for a wild garden.

Culinary uses: Not generally acceptable.

Other uses: Comfrey Tea. Medicinal; has many remarkable healing qualities. Can be very decorative in the garden. There are shorter-growing varieties and an attractive variegated form. Good for the compost heap.

CORIANDER

(Coriandrum sativum)

Description: Annual, dark green divided leaves and pretty clusters of mauve or white flowers in midsummer. Height, 45cm (18in).
Where to grow: Well-drained soil, sunny position.
Propagation: Seeds sown where required to grow.
Sowing time: Spring.
Available fresh: Young leaves can be cut in summer as required.
Harvesting for storage: Drying of leaves not recommended. Freezes well. Seeds usually ready for harvesting in mid- to late summer.

Special tip: Unripe seeds have unpleasant smell.
Flavour: Ripe seeds have spicy, orange tang. Young leaves have distinctive flavour.
Culinary uses: Add crushed or whole ripe seeds to soups, sauces, ratatouille, salad, fish, meat, terrines, chicken, duck and game dishes, (especially those incorporating apples, pears and oranges) and fruity desserts. Use chopped leaves in curries and chutneys, and whole leaves as garnish.
Other uses: None.

COSTMARY

(Chrysanthemum balsamita)

Description: Perennial growing up to 1m (3ft) with grey-green leaves, clusters of small yellow flowers in midsummer.
Where to grow: Well-drained soil in sun and shelter.
Propagation: Division of plants in spring.
Planting time: Autumn or spring.
Available fresh: Young leaves in spring, summer and autumn, some in winter.
Harvesting for storage: Flowers and leaves can be dried in summer as required. Leaves freeze well.

Special tip: A rather untidy plant but well worth growing.
Flavour: Young leaves have sharp, minty flavour. Use sparingly.
Culinary uses: Small amount, finely chopped, can be added to soups, stews, and casseroles of poultry, game and veal. Traditional flavouring for home-brewed ale.
Other uses: Flowers and leaves dried for pot-pourri and herbal sachets. Dried leaves make good book markers. Bruised leaves will ease the pain of bee stings.

COTTON LAVENDER

(Santolina chamaecyparissus)

Description: Shrubby perennial with silver-grey, finely cut leaves through summer and winter. Small yellow button flowers in midsummer. Can reach 75cm (2½ft).
Where to grow: Well-drained soil, open sunny position.
Propagation: Heel cuttings in summer.
Planting time: Spring.
Harvesting for storage: Cut for drying at any time in summer and save any prunings. Flowers may be dried as available and used in winter arrangements.

Special tips: Withstands, drought conditions. Prune overlarge plants in spring. Formal hedges need another pruning in midsummer.
Culinary uses: None.
Other uses: As moth deterrent, place dried sprays among clothes. Sometimes used in pot-pourri. An attractive, useful garden plant, singly or as low hedge. *S. neapolitana* especially pretty for flower arranging. Other good varieties described on page 47.

CUMIN
(*Cuminum cyminum*)

Description: Half-hardy annual with feathery leaves and clusters of tiny white or pink flowers from early to midsummer. Height 30–60cm (1–2ft).

Where to grow: Well-drained soil, sunny position.

Propagation: Seed under glass in early spring and planted out as below, or sown direct into ground in late spring.

Planting time: Late spring.

Available fresh: Seeds in late summer.

Harvesting for storage: Cut stems and dry as seeds begin to ripen.

Special tips: Seeds only ripen in a hot summer. Green seeds have unpleasant taste.

Flavour: Ripe seeds have slightly pungent aniseed flavour.

Culinary uses: Add to spicy Mexican stews, Middle-eastern, Indian and Oriental dishes, pickles, chutneys, curry sauces.

Other uses: Cumin Water. Valuable medicinal qualities.

CURRY PLANT
(*Helichrysum angustifolium*)

Description: Shrubby perennial with all-year, thin, silver, crowded leaves and deep golden button flowers in midsummer. Height about 45cm (18in).

Where to grow: Well-drained soil, sunny and sheltered position.

Propagation: Cuttings in late summer. Keep in cold frame for first winter.

Planting time: Spring.

Available fresh: Leaves in summer.

Harvesting for storage: Sprays can be cut in summer for drying or freezing but do not cut in late summer or autumn as the shoots will die back.

Special tip: A marginally hardy plant and not suitable for colder areas.

Flavour: Distinctive curry flavour.

Culinary uses: Add chopped leaves to sauces, stuffings, scrambled eggs, kromeskies, croquettes of fish, meat and eggs.

Other uses: Sprays hung in cupboards will deter moths. One of the brightest and most attractive silver-leaved plants for the garden.

DILL
(*Anethum graveolens*)

Description: Hardy annual with feathery foliage and clustered yellow flowers in midsummer. Height about 60cm (2ft).

Where to grow: Well-drained soil, sunny sheltered position.

Propagation: Seeds sown where required to grow.

Sowing time: Spring and summer.

Available fresh: Leaves any time from about 2 months after sowing.

Harvesting for storage: Cut seed heads as they brown, but before fully ripe. Leaves freeze well.

Special tip: Never let soil around seedlings dry out at any time.

Flavour: Seeds similar flavour to caraway; leaves different flavour.

Culinary uses: Add seeds to bread, biscuits, pastry, pickles. Use chopped leaves for salads, especially cucumber and tomato, salad dressings, marinades. Sprinkle on egg dishes, cooked vegetables. Add, when finishing, to fish, meat, poultry and game casseroles. Use to make Dill Vinegar. Fresh feathery leaves and yellow flowers are pretty garnish for fish.

Other uses: Medicinal; Dill Water.

ELDER

(*Sambucus nigra*)

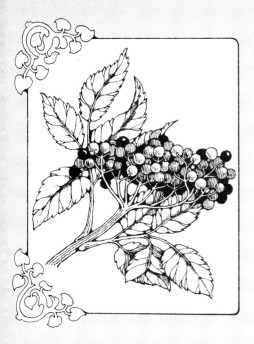

Description: Deciduous shrub or small tree. Flat clusters of cream-coloured flowers and black berries.

Where to grow: Preferably damp soil in sun or part shade.

Propagation: Hardwood cuttings in autumn.

Planting time: Late autumn and winter.

Available fresh: Flowers in early to midsummer; berries in autumn.

Harvesting for storage: Flowers for drying when whole head open.

Special tip: For a decorative garden shrub, grow variety *aurea*.

Flavour: Flowers have honey-muscatel flavour. Berries have stronger, sharper flavour.

Culinary uses: Flowers add a distinctive flavour to preserves, especially gooseberry. Fried in light batter, make delicious fritters. Berries and flowers popular for wine making.

Other uses: Medicinal — Elder Flower Tea; Cosmetic — Elder Flower Water. Enjoyed by bees.

FENNEL

(*Foeniculum vulgare*)

Description: Perennial with feathery green leaves and heads of tiny yellow flowers in mid- to late summer. Height up to 1·5m (5ft). For Florence Fennel, see page 34.

Where to grow: Well-drained, preferably chalky soil. Sunny position.

Propagation: Seed sown outdoors, or division; both in spring.

Planting time: Spring.

Available fresh: Leaves in summer.

Harvesting for storage: Cut leaves for drying just before flowering, but flavour is easily lost. Drying seeds difficult but retain flavour well if successful. Leaves and stems freeze well.

Special tip: Can be kept to about 45cm (18in) by pinching.

Flavour: Seeds have aromatic aniseed flavour; leaves milder.

Culinary uses: Especially good with oily fish, fatty lamb, pork. Use for soups, sauces, salads, salad dressings, stuffings, vegetable dishes. Shoots and stems are used in Provençale dishes.

Other uses: Herbal tea. Decorative garden plant.

GARLIC

(*Allium sativum*)

Description: Perennial from a bulb. Broad flat leaves, occasionally small white flowers. Height, 30–100cm (1–3ft).

Where to grow: Light, well-drained, but rich, soil in full sun.

Propagation: Offsets.

Planting time: Spring, also autumn in warmer parts of the country.

Available fresh: Autumn, from spring planting; mid- to late summer from autumn planting.

Harvesting for storage: Lift bulbs as soon as leaves yellow.

Special tip: Soil should be well dug and not made too firm.

Flavour: Persistent onion flavour.

Culinary uses: Use with discretion, except for addicts. An essential ingredient in many Mediterranean and Eastern dishes. Crush or chop cloves (small bulb offsets) for soups, sauces, soft cheese, fish meat, poultry, Mediterranean vegetables, salads. Use juice to flavour butter, oil, vinegar, salt. Garlic in cooked dishes becomes peppery in freezer, better added later.

Other uses: Valuable medicinal qualities when included in diet.

GERANIUM

(Pelargonium spp.)

Description: Half-hardy perennials. The most popular scented-leaved geraniums are rose and lemon. Both have deeply cut attractive leaves. Flowers in summer, pink or pale lilac. Height, 60cm (2ft).

Where to grow: Cool greenhouse or house in well-drained pots of John Innes or a soilless compost.

Propagation: Cutting indoors in pots in spring, or late summer.

Planting time: Outdoors in late spring, or after frost danger over, in reasonably good, well-drained soil, sunny position.

Available fresh: All summer. A few leaves may be cut in winter.

Harvesting for storage: Leaves may be dried as available in summer.

Special tip: Bring indoors and store free from frost in winter.

Flavour: Leaves are scented according to variety, with lemon, nutmeg, rose and other perfumes.

Culinary uses: Add a few leaves to desserts, preserves, jellies, sorbets, cooked fruit.

Other uses: Herbal tea from fresh or dried leaves; dried leaves in pot-pourri.

HORSERADISH

(Cochlearia armoracia)

Description: Vigorous hardy perennial. Large green leaves on long stalks and 1·25-m (4-ft) spikes of white flowers in summer.

Where to grow: Preferably rich, light but moist soil in sun.

Propagation: Root cuttings, (thongs) 20cm (8in) long inserted outdoors in early spring.

Planting time: Spring or autumn.

Available fresh: Not until second year after planting then remove roots as required.

Harvesting for storage: Roots can be stored in damp sand after lifting. Do not dry.

Special tips: Almost impossible to eradicate once planted. Grow well away from other plants.

Flavour: Hot and pungent but volatile if heated.

Culinary uses: Add grated root to cream (traditionally served with roast beef), seafood cocktail sauce, mayonnaise, hot and cold sauces for smoked fish, chicken salad, Scandinavian and German dishes. Preserve grated root in vinegar.

Other uses: Aids digestion.

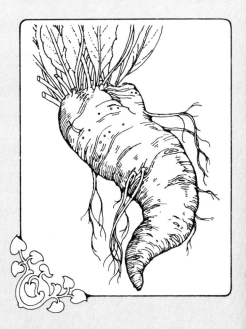

HYSSOP

(Hyssopus officinalis)

Description: Small-leaved, bushy evergreen shrub. Spikes of small flowers, usually deep blue, all summer. Height, 30–60cm (1–2ft).

Where to grow: Light, well-drained soil, sunny position.

Propagation: Seeds sown where required to grow, division or heel cuttings in spring.

Planting time: Spring.

Available fresh: Mainly summer, young growth and flowers.

Harvesting for storage: Dry flower spikes and leaves as available from early to late summer.

Special tip: Can be clipped to make a low hedge.

Flavour: Bitter, use with discretion.

Culinary uses: Leaves can be added sparingly to soups, stews; flowers can be used to garnish salads.

Other uses: Flowers and leaves dried for pot-pourri. Good for bees and butterflies.

JUNIPER
(*Juniperus communis*)

Description: Shrubby, evergreen, aromatic conifer with grey-green leaves. Berries eventually black. Height, 1·25–3·75m (4–12ft).
Where to grow: Ordinary garden soil, sun or light shade.
Propagation: Cuttings in autumn, seed in a cold frame in spring or autumn.
Planting time: Early autumn or spring.
Available fresh: Autumn when berries have turned black.
Harvesting for storage: In autumn. Dry berries until slightly shrivelled.

Special tips: You need a male and female plant to obtain berries. May be more practical to buy them.
Flavour: Ripe berries have aromatic sweet flavour, touched with orange and pine. Dried berries should be crushed.
Culinary uses: Excellent in marinades for game, pork and mutton, and to spiced brine for pickling ham and beef. Use to season pâtés, stuffings, sausages, pork chops, game dishes.
Other uses: Medicinal; Juniper Berry Tea.

LAVENDER
(*Lavandula spica*, syn. *L. officinalis*)

Description: Evergreen shrub with small greyish leaves and spikes of usually purple flowers, midsummer. Height, 60–100cm (2–3ft).
Where to grow: Well-drained soil, sunny position.
Propagation: Heel cuttings will root at any time, but best taken in late summer or early autumn for planting out following spring.
Planting time: Spring.
Available fresh: Flower spikes in midsummer.
Harvesting for storage: Cut flower spikes for drying before flowers open, usually in midsummer.
Special tips: Cut back straggly plants in spring and prune lightly after flowering. Renew from cuttings as necessary.
Flavour: Strongly scented.
Culinary uses: Crystallized flowers make attractive cake decorations.
Other uses: Dried flowers for potpourri, sachets and 'baskets'. A shrub or low hedge for every garden. Enjoyed by bees.

LEMON BALM
(*Melissa officinalis*)

Description: Perennial with tough, green, rounded and wrinkled leaves and spikes of small white flowers in summer. Height, 60cm (2ft).
Where to grow: Preferably good moist soil, sun or part shade.
Propagation: Division outdoors or cuttings under glass, both in spring. Seed sown where required to grow in late spring.
Planting time: Spring or autumn.
Available fresh: Young leaves through spring and summer.
Harvesting for storage: Cut for drying or freezing as flower buds develop for maximum amount of flavour.
Special tips: In cold districts protect with peat or leafmould in winter.
Flavour: Delicate lemon aroma.
Culinary uses: Use with fish, meat, poultry and fruit compotes. Add chopped fresh leaves to salads and soups; whole leaves to wine cups. Crystallize leaves to add to cakes and cold desserts.
Other uses: Tonic herbal tea; bath herb; dried leaves for pot-pourri. Gold and gold variegated varieties attractive garden plants.

LEMON VERBENA
(Lippia citriodora)

Description: Doubtfully hardy shrub. Pretty, light green, pointed leaves and sprays of tiny lilac or white flowers in late summer. Up to 3m (10ft) high.

Where to grow: Well-drained unmanured soil in shelter of south-facing wall. Can be grown in pots and brought into frost-free greenhouse or indoors in winter.

Propagation: Soft or ripe woody cuttings in summer and autumn.

Planting time: Spring.

Available fresh: Leaves in summer or early autumn.

Harvesting for storage: Leaves, stems and flowers can be dried. Leaves retain aroma when frozen. Cut in midsummer as available.

Special tips: Too rich a soil makes the plant less hardy. Needs protection outdoors in winter.

Flavour: Scented lemon flavour.

Culinary uses: Used to flavour sweet sauces, milk puddings, fruit salad, cakes. Sprinkle chopped leaves on cold desserts. Use whole leaves to garnish wine cups.

Other uses: Herbal tea; one of the best plants for pot-pourri.

LOVAGE
(Ligusticum officinale)

Description: Perennial with dark green divided leaves and large heads of tiny greenish flowers in early to midsummer, followed by brown seed heads. Up to 2·5m (8ft) high.

Where to grow: Preferably moist, rich soil in sun or part shade.

Propagation: Division in spring or ripe seeds sown where required to grow in midsummer.

Planting time: Spring or autumn.

Available fresh: Leaves and stems from late spring to late summer. Roots in spring.

Harvesting for storage: Young leaves for drying or freezing and stems for crystallizing in early to midsummer. Cut seed heads just before fully ripe.

Special tip: One plant probably sufficient.

Flavour: Spicy celery flavour.

Culinary uses: Add chopped leaves to soups, sauces, stews, casseroles. Young leaves can be used in salads, seeds on cheese biscuits. Stems and roots are also edible.

Other uses: Medicinal; herbal tea; bath herb.

MARIGOLD
(Calendula officinalis)

Description: Hardy annual with familiar orange or yellow daisy flowers, early summer to autumn. Height, 30cm (12in).

Where to grow: Ordinary soil, sun or light shade.

Propagation: Seeds.

Sowing time: Spring, where required to grow.

Available fresh: Leaves and flower petals in summer.

Harvesting for storage: Pull petals from flowers and dry as available.

Special tip: Cut off dead unused flower heads to prolong flowering period and prevent formation of seeds.

Flavour: Leaves bitter, young leaves palatable.

Culinary uses: Petals make a colourful garnish for salads, both sweet and savoury. The colour can be extracted by simmering petals, and liquid used to colour sweet or savoury dishes.

Other uses: Adds gay colour to herb garden. Medicinal; herbal tea.

MARJORAM, POT
(Origanum onites)

Description: Perennial, spreading mounds of small green leaves and pink or white flowers in mid-summer. Height, 45cm (18in).

Where to grow: Good, light soil, sheltered sunny position.

Propagation: Seed sown where required to grow, or division, both in spring. Cuttings in summer.

Planting time: Spring.

Available fresh: Young sprigs in mid- to late summer.

Harvesting for storage: Main cutting for drying just before flowering. Aroma retained better by freezing rather than drying.

Special tip: Of the several marjorams, pot marjoram is easiest.

Flavour: Sweet thyme-like flavour.

Culinary uses: Add to robust soups, sauces, marinades, basting sauces, stuffings, fish, meat, poultry, game, hot cheese and pasta dishes. Sprinkle on cooked vegetables, raw vegetable salads. Fresh sprigs and flowers make an attractive garnish for salads.

Other uses: Herbal tea; pot-pourri; bath herb. A good bee plant. See also page 48.

MINT
(Mentha spp.)

Description: Perennials with usually green leaves and mauve flowers in summer. Height, 45cm (18in).

Where to grow: Rich, moist soil.

Propagation: Division in autumn or spring; or by runners, removed and planted in summer.

Planting time: Autumn or spring.

Available fresh: Spring to autumn.

Harvesting for storage: Dry or freeze as plants start to flower.

Special tips: Very invasive.

Flavour: Varies according to species.

Culinary uses: Use chopped fresh leaves of apple or spearmint as tasty garnish on soups, cooked vegetables, salads, to flavour savoury butter, mint sauce and jelly for lamb, meat pasties, stuffing for veal and lamb, in yogurt, salad dressings. Use sprigs to flavour vinegar, mint julep, wine cups, fruit drinks. Ginger mint is good in chutneys. Eau de Cologne mint is too perfumed for culinary uses. Leaves can be crystallized.

Other uses: Peppermint Tea; pot-pourri. Variegated apple mint a decorative plant.

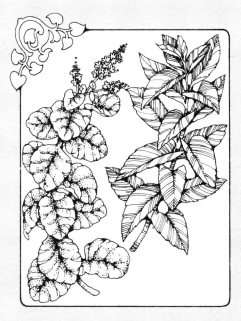

NASTURTIUM
(Tropaeolum majus and T. minus)

Description: Familiar annual with helmet-shaped, spurred flowers of yellow, orange or red in mid- to late summer. Climbing or dwarf.

Where to grow: Well-drained soil, preferably sunny position.

Propagation: Seeds sown outdoors.

Sowing time: Late spring.

Available fresh: Leaves, flowers and seeds in summer.

Harvesting for storage: For drying, cut leaves in early to midsummer before flowering.

Special tips: Grow in richer soil if leaves are required in quantity. May get blackfly in summer months.

Flavour: Similar to capers. Young leaves peppery, seeds are more pungent, buds milder.

Culinary uses: Chopped young leaves good in sandwiches, especially with cream cheese and in salads. Fresh petals make edible salad garnish. Use pickled buds and seeds in sauces, stuffings.

Other uses: Climbing varieties useful quick cover for fences and banks. Dwarf varieties for edging or front of border. Medicinal: Valuable source of vitamin C.

PARSLEY
(Petroselinum crispum)

Description: Biennial. Fresh green, finely cut and usually crinkled leaves. Height about 13cm (5in).
Where to grow: Good soil in sun or part shade.
Propagation: Seed usually sown where required to grow in spring and summer.
Planting time: Spring and summer.
Available fresh: All year if given protection of cloche in winter.
Harvesting for storage: Drying not recommended, freezes well.
Special tips: Soak seeds overnight before sowing.

Flavour: Very popular, blends well with other herbs.
Culinary uses: Essential ingredient in bouquet garni, Maître d'Hôtel Butter. Add chopped leaves to soups, stocks, marinades, sauces, salad dressings, fish, meat, poultry, game, egg dishes, stuffings. Lavish addition of chopped fresh leaves will give sauces and soups strong green colour. Use sprigs as garnish.
Other uses: Rich source of vitamins and minerals; Parsley Tea recommended for rheumatism. For Hamburg parsley, see page 39.

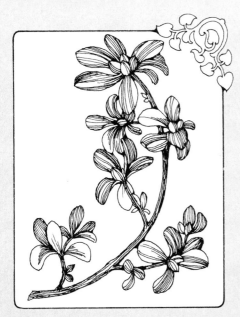

PURSLANE
(Portulaca oleracea)

Description: Annual with reddish stems and small fleshy leaves. Yellow flowers in midsummer. Height, 15cm (6in).
Where to grow: Light, rich soil, open sunny position.
Propagation: Seed sown direct into garden in late spring or in early spring under cloches.
Planting time: Spring.
Available fresh: Young shoots in summer.
Harvesting for storage: Not recommended for drying. Freezes well.
Special tips: Keep cutting to encourage further growth. Use only the leaves and discard the stems.
Flavour: Sharp, slightly nutty flavour. Use leaves sparingly.
Culinary uses: Young leaves can be added to salads or cooked like sorrel. Fleshy leaves can be pickled.
Other uses: A pretty edging plant. Golden-leaved variety particularly recommended though not quite so hardy.

ROSEMARY
(Rosmarinus officinalis)

Description: Evergreen shrub with spiky leaves and pale violet flowers in spring. Up to 2m (6ft) high.
Where to grow: Well-drained soil, sunny sheltered position.
Propagation: Cuttings, from midsummer to early autumn.
Planting time: Spring.
Available fresh: All year.
Harvesting for storage: Cut for drying or freezing, preferably in late summer.
Special tip: Best against a wall.
Flavour: Aromatic, fairly pungent. Agreeable but use with discretion.

Culinary uses: Infuse sprigs in marinades, basting sauces, soups, sauces, casseroles, and withdraw before serving. Insert sprigs in roasting chicken, lamb and pork. Chop finely fresh leaves, or crush dried, and add to stuffings, basting sauces, savoury butter for grilled fish, meat, poultry, game.
Other uses: Rosemary Tea; for hairwashing and bath; pot-pourri. For other good garden varieties see pages 47 and 48.

RUE
(*Ruta graveolens*)

Description: Evergreen, semi-woody shrub. Beautifully cut and shaped blue-green leaves. Tiny greenish-yellow flowers, early to late summer. Height about 60cm (2ft).
Where to grow: Well-drained soil, sunny position.
Propagation: Seeds sown where required to grow in spring, or cuttings in midsummer.
Planting time: Spring.
Available fresh: All year.
Harvesting for storage: Not recommended.

Special tip: Prune back straggly shoots in late spring to encourage bushy growth.
Flavour: Usually considered too bitter for culinary use.
Other uses: Crushed leaves rubbed on to skin will relieve pain of bee stings and rheumatism. A most decorative garden plant particularly the form Jackman's Blue, and also the variegated variety when available. Leaves useful for flower arrangement.

SAGE
(*Salvia officinalis*)

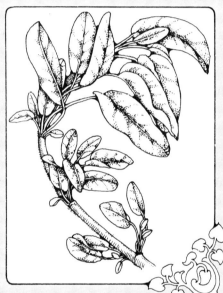

Description: Evergreen shrub with rough, greyish leaves. Up to 60cm (2ft) high.
Where to grow: Well-drained soil, sunny sheltered position.
Propagation: Heel cuttings from spring to autumn; layering in spring.
Planting time: Spring.
Available fresh: Almost all year.
Harvesting for storage: Cut in early and late summer for drying or freezing.
Special tip: Grow broad-leaved rather than narrow-leaved form.

Flavour: Strong, aromatic flavour.
Culinary uses: Add chopped fresh leaves to robust soups, sauces, stuffings (for veal in Italy, traditionally in England for pork, duck, goose), meat, poultry and game dishes. Use with cooked vegetables, especially green and butter beans, stuffed onions and tomatoes. Fresh leaves are used in making Sage Derby cheese. Sprigs and flowers make attractive garnish. Add also to cream cheese.
Other uses: Sage Tea as tonic. For other varieties, see page 47.

SALAD BURNET
(*Sanguisorba minor*)

Description: Perennial with charming double rows of tiny green leaves and rounded greenish flower heads, early to late summer. Height about 30cm (1ft).
Where to grow: Any average soil, sun or part shade.
Propagation: Seed sown where required to grow in spring. Division of roots, spring or autumn.
Planting time: Spring or autumn.
Available fresh: All year.
Special tips: Remove flower heads and keep; cut back to about 15cm (6in) to ensure supply of young leaves. Probably the easiest herb to grow.
Flavour: Young leaves have cucumber flavour; mature leaves bitter.
Culinary uses: Cook chopped leaves in delicate soups, sauces with fish, chicken, veal. Use raw in salads, salad dressings or delicate cooked vegetables like chard, asparagus, seakale, artichokes. Use whole leaves in wine cups, fruit drinks in place of borage.
Other uses: Worth growing if only for its decorative leaves. Makes a very pretty pot plant.

SAVORY, WINTER
(Satureja montana)

Description: Shrubby perennial with tiny, dark, evergreen leaves and small white to purplish flowers in mid- to late summer. Height, 30cm (1ft).

Where to grow: Light, even poor soil; full sun.

Propagation: Seeds sown where required to grow, or division, both in spring. Heel cuttings in spring and summer.

Planting time: Spring or autumn.

Available fresh: All year.

Special tip: In cold districts cover with cloche, or pot up for indoor growing in the winter months.

Flavour: Piquant, fairly strong flavour.

Culinary uses: Pleasant alternative to sage in robust soups, sauces, stuffings for pork, veal, turkey, duck, game, casseroles. Excellent with green beans, haricot beans, lentils, split peas. Can be used in marinades and basting sauces with other herbs.

Other uses: Decorative plant for front of herb border or rock garden. For summer savory, see page 42. Both enjoyed by bees.

SORREL, FRENCH
(Rumex scutatus)

Description: Perennial. Green arrow-shaped leaves (resembling spinach) and green flower heads in summer. Height about 30cm (1ft).

Where to grow: Light, rich, preferably acid soil, sun or part shade.

Propagation: Division of roots, spring or autumn. Seed sown where required to grow in spring.

Planting time: Spring or autumn.

Available fresh: Summer to autumn as soon as plant has four or five leaves.

Harvesting for storage: Leaves can be gathered for drying and freezing just before flowering time.

Special tips: Wild sorrel (*R. acetosa*) can also be used.

Flavour: Slightly bitter, use with discretion, especially wild sorrel.

Culinary uses: Add a few young leaves to potato and green salads. Cook with lettuce, in potato, haricot bean and pea soup. Use sorrel puree (cook covered, slowly without water, like spinach) in omelettes, sauces for fish.

Other uses: None.

SOUTHERNWOOD
(Artemisia abrotanum)

Description: Hardy shrub with fragrant thread-like grey leaves in thick clusters. (Rarely flowers, even in southern England.) Height to 1m (3ft).

Where to grow: Well-drained soil, open sunny position.

Propagation: Cuttings in spring or midsummer in cold frame.

Planting time: Spring.

Available fresh: Leafy sprays in summer for arrangements and nosegays.

Harvesting for storage: If required for drying, cut stems in midsummer and dry in usual way.

Special tip: In spring, cut back last year's growth to two or three buds.

Flavour: Bitter, not suitable for cooking.

Other uses: Can be dried for potpourri; sprays among clothes will deter moths; used alone or with hops for herb pillows. A decorative garden shrub and flower arranger's plant both for scent and grey shaggy leaves.

SWEET CICELY
(Myrrhis odorata)

Description: Perennial. Beautiful light green, fern-like leaves and small white flowers in early summer. Height up to 1·5m (5ft).
Where to grow: Good, well-drained moist soil in part shade.
Propagation: Division of roots in spring or autumn; seed sown where required to grow in spring.
Planting time: Spring or autumn.
Available fresh: All the year round except in midwinter.
Harvesting for storage: Drying of leaves difficult, but seeds can be dried and used finely crushed.

Special tips: Remove flower heads if only leaves required.
Flavour: Sweet, faintly aniseed flavour.
Culinary uses: Fresh-chopped leaves and stalks, or 2 or 3 teaspoons dried leaves, added to stewed fruit and tarts, saves sugar. Add chopped fresh leaves to green and fruit salads. Young roots can be boiled and dressed with Vinaigrette Sauce. Leaves make attractive garnish for sauces.
Other uses: Dried flowers used in pot-pourri.

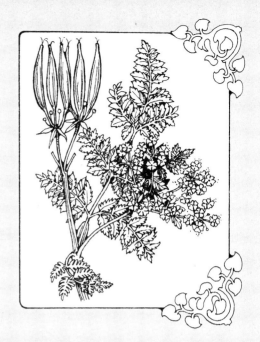

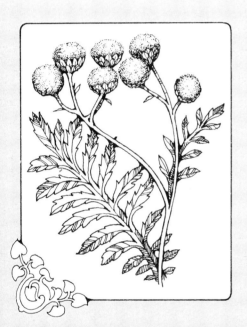

TANSY
(Tanacetum vulgare)

Description: A perennial with pretty, finely cut, sometimes curled green leaves. Yellow button flowers in clusters in mid- to late summer. Height, 60–100cm (2–3ft).
Where to grow: Ordinary garden soil, sun or part shade.
Propagation: Division of roots in spring, autumn or winter.
Planting time: Spring, autumn or winter.
Available fresh: Leaves from spring to autumn. Late-summer flowers for indoor decorations.
Harvesting for storage: Flower heads can be dried for winter arrangements.

Special tips: A very invasive plant which must not be allowed to spread too much.
Flavour: Aromatic, rather bitter.
Culinary uses: Finely chopped young leaves are used sparingly to flavour old-fashioned English Tansy Pudding and Tansy Custard.
Other uses: Not recommended medicinally. Large doses are poisonous. Pretty border plant especially the curled-leaf variety, and useful for flower arranging.

TARRAGON, FRENCH
(Artemisia dracunculus var: sativa)

Description: Perennial with branching stems and narrow, pointed leaves. Flowers white, early to midsummer. Height, 60–100cm (2–3ft).
Where to grow: Well-drained soil enriched with humus, sunny position.
Propagation: Division in spring.
Planting time: Spring.
Available fresh: Early summer to autumn.
Harvesting for storage: Drying not recommended, but freezes well.
Special tips: Grow French and not Russian variety which has little flavour. Protect with straw, leafmould or peat in winter.

Flavour: Fresh leaves of French tarragon have delightful aromatic flavour.
Culinary uses: Add chopped fresh leaves to soups, stuffings, sauces for fish, meat, poultry, vegetables and egg dishes. Use to flavour vinegar, mustard, salad dressings, butter for grilling. Sprinkle chopped leaves on fish, chicken and vegetable salads for flavour and garnish.
Other uses: None.

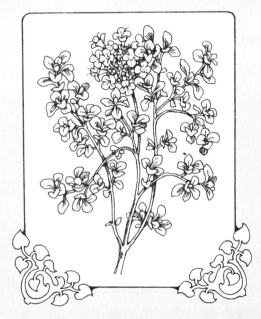

THYME

(*Thymus vulgaris*) Garden Thyme, (*T. citriodorus*) Lemon Thyme

Description: Bushy evergreen shrublet with tiny green leaves and small lilac flowers in mid-summer. Height about 23cm (9in).

Where to grow: Good, well-drained soil, sunny position.

Propagation: Division or layering in spring.

Planting time: Preferably spring.

Available fresh: Sprigs for cutting late spring to early autumn.

Harvesting for storage: Cut for drying or freezing when flowering.

Special tip: Lemon thyme is less hardy than garden thyme.

Flavour: Leaves aromatic.

Culinary uses: Essential ingredient of bouquet garni. Use chopped leaves in sauces, marinades, basting sauces, stuffings, casseroles, fish, meat, poultry, game and pasta dishes. Sprinkle on salads and cooked vegetables.

Other uses: Thyme Tea; pot-pourri; herb baths. Good bee plant for flavouring honey. Gold and silver leaved varieties ideal for rock garden, see page 51. Wild English thyme for lawns, see page 51.

WOODRUFF

(*Asperula odorata*)

Description: Dwarf perennial with 'ruffs' or green leaves on 15-cm (6-in) stems, and clusters of tiny white flowers in early summer.

Where to grow: Preferably damp soil in shade or semi-shade. Likes chalk soils.

Propagation: Division of plants in spring.

Planting time: Spring.

Available fresh: Spring, summer.

Harvesting for storage: For drying best cut in spring just before, or during, flowering.

Special tip: Scent only develops as the leaves begin to dry out.

Flavour: Scent of new-mown hay.

Culinary uses: Used to flavour German · Mai Bowle (wine cup made with Rhine or Mosel wine and strawberries). Not used for cooking.

Other uses: Medicinally as herbal tea; used in pot-pourri and herb pillows. Dried sprays will remove mustiness from cupboards and closed bookcases. A pretty ground cover plant for shade.

WORMWOOD

(*Artemisia absinthium*)

Description: Shrubby perennial with finely cut, silver-grey, aromatic leaves and large sprays of small brownish balled flowers in mid-summer. Height 60cm (2ft), or more when in flower.

Where to grow: Well-drained soil, sunny position.

Propagation: Division or cuttings in spring.

Planting time: Spring.

Available fresh: Foliage in summer for flower arrangement.

Harvesting for storage: If required for drying, cut in midsummer or as available during rest of year.

Special tip: Grow variety called Lambrook Silver.

Flavour: Very bitter, not suitable for cooking.

Other uses: Sprays hung in a room will keep away flies. Dried sprays laid in clothes will repel moths. One of the best silver-leaved plants for the garden, attractive even in winter.

Lamb kebabs with rice salad ring (see page 87)

VII
Cooking with Herbs

ANGELICA

All parts of this plant are edible and both the leaves and stems have a subtle muscatel flavour. The fresh leaves give a fragrant taste to fruit compotes and cold drinks, but it is the pretty green crystallized stems which are most in demand for decorating and flavouring cakes and desserts. Crystallized angelica is expensive to buy so it is worthwhile making your own. Choose only the young flower stems while they are green and tender and cut them 8–15 cm/3–6 inches long.

To crystallize angelica
(Simple method)

METRIC/IMPERIAL/AMERICAN
450g/1lb/1lb young angelica stalks
50g/2oz/¼ cup salt dissolved in 600ml/
   1 pint/2½ cups water

450g/1lb/1lb granulated sugar
about 300ml/½ pint/1¼ cups water
sugar for glazing

Trim the leaves off the angelica stalks and soak in the salted water for 10 minutes. Rinse, drop into fresh boiling water and simmer gently until tender. Drain carefully and scrape off the outer skin. Spread half the sugar on a large dish, lay the angelica stems on top and spread over the remaining sugar. Cover and leave for 2 days.

Put the sugar in a saucepan with the 300ml/½ pint/1¼ cups water, heat gently until dissolved. Put in the angelica and simmer gently until semi-transparent. The stems must be covered, so add a little water if it has evaporated too much. When transparent, drain the angelica thoroughly and roll each piece in granulated sugar. Put on a wire cake rack and finish drying in a cool oven or airing cupboard. Cool thoroughly and store in a dark, airtight container to preserve the colour and flavour. It may not keep quite so long as the commercially processed angelica, which takes several days to make, but it is very good.

Russian paskha

METRIC/IMPERIAL/AMERICAN
100g/4oz/½ cup unsalted butter
100g/4oz/½ cup castor sugar
2 egg yolks
¼ teaspoon vanilla essence
225g/8oz/1 cup medium fat curd cheese
50g/2oz/⅓ cup glacé angelica, chopped

50g/2oz/⅓ cup glacé pineapple, chopped
50g/2oz/¼ cup glacé cherries
3 tablespoons/3 tablespoons/¼ cup
   sultanas
25g/1oz/¼ cup almonds or walnuts,
   chopped

In Russia, Paskha is traditionally served at Easter and is made in a special wooden pyramid shape, but a plastic flower pot is a handy substitute. It is a delicious sweet to eat at any time of the year.

Cream the butter, sugar, egg yolks and vanilla essence until light. Sieve the curd cheese and gradually beat into the creamed mixture. Fold in the angelica, glacé fruits, sultanas and nuts. Line a plastic flower pot or colander with damp muslin and press in the mixture. Cover with a saucer or small plate and put a weight on top. Leave for 24 hours and unmould on to a serving platter. If you have used a colander, you can shape the Paskha into the traditional pyramid shape with a palette knife before decorating with glacé fruits and walnuts. Serve with fresh fruit or cold fruit compote.

Angelica and walnut cakes

METRIC/IMPERIAL/AMERICAN
75g/3oz/6 tablespoons butter
75g/3oz/6 tablespoons castor sugar
grated rind and juice of 1 orange
1 large egg, beaten
150g/5oz/1¼ cups self-raising flour
3 tablespoons/3 tablespoons/¼ cup angelica, chopped

25g/1oz/¼ cup walnuts, chopped
Topping:
75g/3oz/¾ cup icing sugar, sifted
walnut quarters
angelica pieces

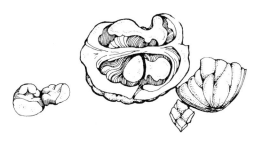

Cream the butter, sugar and 1 teaspoon orange rind until light and fluffy. Gradually beat in the egg. Fold in the sifted flour and 1 tablespoon orange juice. Fold in the angelica and walnuts. Using a teaspoon, half fill 12 greased patty pans and bake just above the centre of a preheated moderately hot oven (200°C, 400°F, Gas Mark 6) for 10–15 minutes until well risen and golden. Turn on to a wire tray to cool. Add sufficient of the remaining orange juice to the icing sugar to make a spreading consistency. When the cakes are cold, coat the tops with the glacé icing and decorate with walnut and angelica pieces.

Angelica garnish

When using crystallized angelica to make stems and leaves for decoration for cold desserts and cakes, open the stems and wash off the glazing sugar to make it more pliable. Dry well before using. Slit thick pieces in half before cutting into shapes for delicate patterns.

BASIL

The sweet, slightly peppery taste of this herb is particularly good with tomatoes, whether they are raw in salads or cooked in the robust dishes of Southern France and Italy.

Soupe au pistou

METRIC/IMPERIAL/AMERICAN
225g/8oz/8oz French beans
225g/8oz/8oz tomatoes, peeled and chopped
225g/8oz/8oz potatoes, peeled and chopped
1 large onion, chopped
1 stick celery, finely chopped
salt and ground black pepper to taste

50g/2oz/2oz vermicelli
3 cloves garlic, peeled
1 handful fresh basil leaves
1 ripe tomato, peeled and sieved
2–3 tablespoons/2–3 tablespoons/3–4 tablespoons olive oil
4 tablespoons/4 tablespoons/⅓ cup grated cheese

Top and tail the beans and chop into 2·5-cm/1-inch lengths. Drop into 1·75 litres/3 pints/4 pints boiling water with the tomatoes, potatoes, onion and celery. Season to taste with the salt and freshly ground black pepper. Simmer steadily for 30 minutes until the vegetables are softened. Add the vermicelli and continue simmering for 15 minutes.

Meanwhile, make a paste (called pistou) by pounding in a mortar the garlic with the basil leaves and sieved tomato, or blend in the liquidizer. When smooth, gradually blend in the olive oil. Stir in about 3 tablespoons of the soup liquor and blend this mixture back into the soup. Adjust the seasoning. Stir in the grated cheese or serve separately at the table.

Liptauer cream cheese (see page 91)

Veal chops Marengo

METRIC/IMPERIAL/AMERICAN

4 veal chops
4 tablespoons/4 tablespoons/⅓ cup
   seasoned flour
2 tablespoons/2 tablespoons/ 3 tablespoons olive oil
50g/2oz/¼ cup butter or margarine
1 medium onion, sliced
1 clove garlic
175g/6oz/6oz mushrooms

100ml/4fl oz/½ cup white wine
1 teaspoon dried basil or 2 teaspoons
   chopped fresh basil
450g/1lb/1lb tomatoes, skinned, or
   1 medium can Italian tomatoes
about 300ml/½ pint/1¼ cups stock or
   water
salt and ground black pepper
1 teaspoon sugar

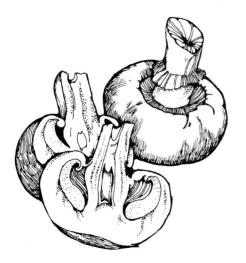

Trim and flour the chops. Heat the olive oil and butter and fry the onion, garlic and mushrooms until the onion is transparent. Add the wine and basil and simmer for 1 minute, then add the tomatoes. Add the meat and sufficient stock or water to cover. Season to taste with salt, black pepper and sugar. Cover and simmer very gently on top of the cooker or in a moderate oven (160°C, 325°F, Gas Mark 3) for 45 minutes or until the meat is tender. When cooked, remove the chops to a heated serving platter and keep warm. Increase the heat to reduce the sauce until slightly thickened and pour over the chops. Garnish with triangles of bread, fried crisp in oil, glazed onions and button mushrooms. If available, sprinkle over a little chopped fresh basil. Serve with fluffy boiled rice, pasta or new potatoes.

Note: You can make this dish very successfully with 700g/1½lb/1½lb of the less expensive stewing veal cut into neat pieces and cooked for about 30 minutes longer; or with chicken joints.

Leeks niçoise

METRIC/IMPERIAL/AMERICAN

4 medium leeks
2 tablespoons/2 tablespoons/3 tablespoons olive oil
225g/8oz/8oz ripe tomatoes or
   canned Italian tomatoes
1 clove garlic
1 teaspoon dried basil or
   1 tablespoon chopped fresh basil

salt and freshly ground pepper
1 teaspoon sugar
lemon juice to taste
Garnish:
chopped fresh basil or parsley

Cut the roots off the leeks and shorten the green tops, leaving about 5cm/2 inches of the leaves. Peel off any that are coarse or discoloured. Make two criss-cross cuts down the centre of the green part of the leeks and plunge them up and down (green part downwards) in cold water until all the grit is removed. Drain and dry on soft kitchen paper.

Heat the olive oil in a shallow flameproof casserole or sauté pan and fry the leeks lightly, turning once.

Skin and chop the raw tomatoes and add with the chopped or crushed garlic and the basil. Season to taste with salt, black pepper and sugar. Cover and cook gently on top of the cooker or in a moderate oven (160°C, 325°F, Gas Mark 3) for 30 minutes or until the leeks are tender. Test by inserting a skewer at the root end. Sharpen to taste with lemon juice and adjust the seasoning. If the sauce is too thin, remove the leeks and keep warm while you reduce the sauce by cooking briskly, uncovered. Serve the leeks in the sauce, garnished with chopped fresh basil or parsley.

BAY

Fresh bay leaves are fairly large and tough and are used whole, infused in fish or meat stock, soups, sauces, marinades, casseroles and stews and then discarded. They have such a strong aroma that one leaf is normally sufficient to flavour 0·5–1 litre/1–2 pints/1¼–2½ pints of liquid. The dried leaves are less potent and are sometimes used crushed. For puddings and sweet sauces, a leaf is heated slowly in the milk used to make the dessert.

For garnishing: wash and dry the fresh leaves and place on top of pâtés, terrines, stuffed tomatoes, rice borders for curries and on kebab skewers.

Lamb kebabs
with rice salad ring
Illustrated on page 81

METRIC/IMPERIAL/AMERICAN
700g/1½lb/1½lb lean shoulder of lamb
4 lambs' kidneys (optional)
175g/6oz/6oz mushrooms
1 large or 2 small green peppers
1 large onion
12 fresh bay leaves
Marinade:
4 tablespoons/4 tablespoons/⅓ cup olive oil
5 tablespoons/5 tablespoons/6 tablespoons lemon juice

1 tablespoon chopped onion
1 clove garlic, crushed
1 teaspoon salt
6 black peppercorns, crushed
pinch ground nutmeg or mace
6 coriander seeds, crushed
2 bay leaves, fresh or dried
sprig thyme or 1 teaspoon dried thyme
sprig mint or 1 teaspoon dried mint
Garnish:
4 sprigs fresh bay or mint

Cut the meat into chunks the size of large walnuts, removing fat and skin, and put into a bowl. (If using kidneys, skin, slit and remove core.) Mix together the ingredients for the marinade and pour over the meat. Leave if possible for 3–4 hours to marinate, turning from time to time.

Wash the mushrooms and cut off stalks. Halve the peppers and discard the seeds and membrane. Cut into pieces roughly the same size as the meat chunks. Peel and quarter the onion.

To cook, oil 4 kebab skewers 30cm/12 inches long. Drain the meat, divide into 4 portions and thread on to the skewers, alternating with pieces of onion, pepper, mushrooms and bay. Cook under a hot grill or over charcoal for 10–15 minutes, turning frequently, until the meat is crisp and brown outside, but still juicy.

To serve, cut a grapefruit or small cabbage heart in half, place cut side down inside the centre of the rice ring and stick in the skewers fanwise. Garnish the skewer handles with fresh bay leaf sprigs in winter or mint in summer, if liked.

Rice salad ring

METRIC/IMPERIAL/AMERICAN
225g/8oz/generous cup long-grain rice
2 tablespoons/2 tablespoons/3 tablespoons chopped chervil or parsley
4 teaspoons snipped chives
1 teaspoon chopped fresh basil or ½ teaspoon dried basil
4 tomatoes, skinned and chopped
8 green olives, chopped
1 small red pimento, scalded or canned

3 tablespoons/3 tablespoons/¼ cup tarragon vinegar
6 tablespoons/6 tablespoons/½ cup olive oil
salt and freshly ground black pepper
lemon juice to taste
Garnish:
6–8 black olives

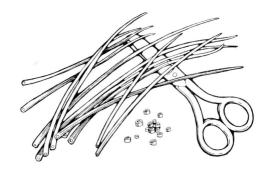

Cook the rice in plenty of boiling salted water for 12 minutes or until just tender. Drain in a colander and cover with a cloth to dry off and keep warm.

Mix together the herbs, chopped tomatoes and olives and stir into the rice. Cut 6 or 8 narrow strips from the pimento, reserving them for garnish, chop up the remainder and add to the rice. Mix together the vinegar, oil and season well with salt and freshly ground pepper. Add sufficient to the rice mixture to moisten it well. Adjust the seasoning and sharpen to taste with lemon juice. Press the rice into 20-cm/8-inch ring mould and leave for 10 minutes or longer before turning out. Place a warm serving plate over the ring, hold both firmly together and invert. Give a quick shake and gently remove the mould. Garnish with pimento strips and stoned black olives.

Serve hot with kebabs (see previous recipe) or cold with the centre filled with chicken, fish or shellfish in mayonnaise or mousseline sauce.

Leeks à la grecque (see page 98)

BORAGE

The pretty blue flowers of this plant make an attractive edible garnish on summer dishes and can be crystallized. The leaves have a pleasant cucumber flavour, but only the young leaves can be used as when they mature they grow bristles and are not palatable. The young leaves can be fried in batter or chopped and added to salads or cream cheese. Leaves and flowers are floated in wine and cider cups and a sprig of borage is traditionally placed in a glass of Pimms No.1. The stems can be skinned and finely chopped and used to flavour salads or cooked vegetables such as cabbage.

Borage fritters

METRIC/IMPERIAL/AMERICAN
bunch young borage leaves
100g/4oz/1 cup plain flour
¼ teaspoon salt
1 egg, separated

175ml/6fl oz/¾ cup water
oil or fat for deep frying
salt

Wash and dry the leaves between soft paper or cloth. Sieve the flour and salt. Make a well in the centre and drop in the egg yolk. Stir in the water a little at a time, gradually drawing the flour in from the sides of the well. Give the batter a good whisk to aerate it. Just before cooking, whisk the egg white until stiff but not brittle and fold into the batter.

Heat the oil or fat to 190°C/375°F. Dip the leaves into the batter, one at a time, and fry until crisp and golden. Drain on soft kitchen paper. Sprinkle with salt and serve with grilled or fried fish or chicken.

Badminton wine cup
with borage

METRIC/IMPERIAL/AMERICAN
½ cucumber
juice of 1 lemon
about 75–100g/3–4oz/1 cup icing sugar
pinch nutmeg or powdered mace
1½ tablespoons/1½ tablespoons/2 tablespoons orange curaçao

1 bottle claret
2–3 sprigs borage
1 bottle soda water
Decoration:
1 orange and/or 1 lemon

Wipe the cucumber, cut into 2 or 3 pieces and put into a punch bowl. Add the lemon juice, sugar, spice, curaçao and claret. Stir from time to time until the sugar has dissolved. Add the borage and chill. When required, add the soda water and ice. Cut 2 or 3 slices of fresh orange and/or lemon and float on top of the bowl with the borage leaves.

Note: Badminton cup is traditionally made with claret but an alternative red wine can be used. The amount of soda used can be varied to taste.

CARAWAY

The seeds of this plant have a strong aniseed flavour and in central Europe are often mixed into meat and vegetable dishes. The young leaves, which are not quite so pungent, are added to salads. In Britain the seeds are more often used in sweet biscuits and old-fashioned seed cake.

Austrian cabbage

METRIC/IMPERIAL/AMERICAN
1 small cabbage, about 450g/1lb/1lb
25–50g/1–2oz/2–4 tablespoons butter or
bacon fat
1 small onion, chopped

1 teaspoon mild paprika
1 teaspoon caraway seeds
salt and ground black pepper to taste
150ml/¼ pint/⅔ cup soured cream

Discard the outer coarse leaves of the cabbage and cut into quarters, remove the stalk. Shred the cabbage finely, wash and drain thoroughly dry in a clean towel.

In a flameproof casserole, heat the butter or fat and fry the onion gently until transparent. Add the shredded cabbage and sauté lightly, stirring well. Sprinkle in the paprika, caraway seeds, salt and freshly ground black pepper. Mix in the soured cream. If this is not available you can sour 150ml/¼ pint/⅔ cup double cream with 1 tablespoon lemon juice.

Cover the casserole and continue cooking very gently on top of the cooker or in a moderate oven (160°C, 325°F, Gas Mark 3) for 15–20 minutes until cabbage is tender. Serve with Hungarian goulash, Bratwurst, grilled sausages or mackerel.

Scots seed cake

METRIC/IMPERIAL/AMERICAN
100g/4oz/½ cup butter or margarine
100g/4oz/½ cup castor sugar
2 eggs, beaten
175g/6oz/1½ cups self-raising flour
¼ teaspoon ground cinnamon
¼ teaspoon ground nutmeg

1 teaspoon caraway seeds
50g/2oz/⅓ cup chopped candied peel
Topping:
2 teaspoons granulated sugar
1 teaspoon caraway seeds

Line and grease a 15–18-cm/6–7-inch cake tin. Cream the butter and sugar until light and fluffy. Gradually beat in the eggs. Sift the flour with the cinnamon and nutmeg and fold into the creamed mixture. Sprinkle in the caraway seeds and mix in with the candied peel.

Turn the mixture into the prepared tin, smooth the top. Mix the granulated sugar and caraway seeds together and sprinkle over cake. Bake in the centre of a preheated moderate oven (160°C, 325°F, Gas Mark 3) for 1 hour or until golden and set. Test with a skewer which will come out clean when the cake is ready. Allow the cake to shrink slightly from the sides of the tin and turn on to a wire rack to cool.

METRIC/IMPERIAL/AMERICAN
100g/4oz/½ cup softened butter
100g/4oz/½ cup low fat curd cheese
½ teaspoon Continental mustard
1–2 teaspoons mild paprika

½ teaspoon chopped caraway seeds
1 teaspoon chopped chives
½ teaspoon chopped capers
salt and black pepper to taste

Liptauer cream cheese

Illustrated on pages 84–5

Cream the butter. Sieve and gradually beat in the cheese. Mix in the other ingredients, adjusting the amount of the individual items to suit your own taste. You can also add a dash of anchovy essence and use chopped spring onions instead of the chives. The cheese is meant to be highly seasoned and pink in colour.

When the mixture is well blended, pile into a dish and garnish with radishes and celery sprigs or watercress. Serve with thinly cut and buttered wholemeal or rye bread or crisp plain biscuits. Liptauer cheese can also be piped onto pastry biscuits for cocktail canapés or used in Scandinavian open sandwiches.

CHERVIL

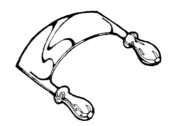

This herb with its delicate aniseed flavour is one of the four which combine to make the classic 'fines herbes' mixture of the French kitchen. The others, used in equal quantities, are parsley, tarragon and chives. Because chervil blends so happily with other herbs it is often used in making sauces and salad dressings. The leaves lose their flavour when dried and should be used fresh or frozen. They also wilt rather quickly, so for garnish should be added just before serving, preferably chopped. The little tufts called 'pluches' are floated on cups of consommé and cold soup and used to garnish cold fish dishes. It is inadvisable to use them on hot dishes as they so soon look sad.

Left: *Grilled salmon steaks with dill cream sauce (see page 106)*

Below: *Provençale fish soup (see page 111)*

93

Omelette fines herbes

METRIC/IMPERIAL/AMERICAN
2 eggs
1 tablespoon water
1 teaspoon chopped chervil
1 teaspoon chopped parsley
1 teaspoon chopped tarragon

1 teaspoon chopped chives
salt and pepper to taste
1 teaspoon butter
Garnish:
parsley sprig

Whisk the eggs well with a fork, a whisk is apt to make them too fluffy for a savoury omelette. Add the water, chopped herbs and season to taste. Heat the butter in a small omelette pan until sizzling, pour in the egg mixture and cook quickly, lifting the setting egg round the edge and running in the liquid egg underneath. When nearly set, but still slightly liquid in the centre, using a palette knife flip one half of the omelette over the other and tip the omelette out quickly on to the warm serving plate. Garnish with a sprig of parsley.

Serve with fresh green salad and French dressing, grilled tomato halves and mushroom caps cooked with herb butter (see page 126).

METRIC/IMPERIAL/AMERICAN
2 teaspoons chopped chervil
1 teaspoon chopped chives
1 teaspoon chopped parsley
300ml/½ pint/1¼ cups consommé or good
    stock

2 whole eggs and 3 yolks
175ml/6fl oz/¾ cup double cream
25g/1oz/¼ cup Parmesan cheese, grated
50g/2oz/½ cup Gruyère or Cheddar
    cheese, grated

Savoury royale custards

Add the herbs to the consommé or stock and heat very gradually to boiling point so the flavours are infused. Beat the eggs together with 2 tablespoons/2 tablespoons/3 tablespoons cream and slowly pour in the boiling liquid, stirring steadily.

Butter 4–6 small dariole moulds and fill with the custard, straining out the herbs. Put in a roasting tin with a 2·5-cm/1-inch depth of water and place in a preheated moderate oven (180°C, 350°F, Gas Mark 4). Cover the moulds with a sheet of buttered greaseproof paper and cook for about 45 minutes or until set. Alternatively, poach in a shallow pan over a low heat. When set, cool and refrigerate until required.

To serve, well butter a shallow flameproof dish and unmould the custards. If preferred, they may be unmoulded into individual heatproof dishes. Heat the remaining cream and pour it over the custards and sprinkle generously with the grated cheese. Place in the top of a hot oven or under the grill until golden. Serve immediately with cress or cucumber sandwiches made with thinly buttered brown bread, for a first course or, if preferred, as a savoury at the end of dinner.

CHIVES

The thin grass-like leaves of chives with their mild onion flavour are best snipped with scissors for garnishing, or finely chopped for flavouring delicate sauces and dishes for which onion is too strong. They are particularly suitable for flavouring salads, cold soups, sauces and many vegetables. They are invariably included in the combination of green herbs called 'fines herbes'.

METRIC/IMPERIAL/AMERICAN
1 large cucumber
25g/1oz/2 tablespoons butter
1 tablespoon snipped chives

salt and freshly ground black pepper to
    taste

Casseroled cucumber
with chives

Cut the cucumber in slices about 2·5cm/1 inch thick. Peel and, if the cucumber is very mature, remove the seeds as they taste bitter. Well butter a casserole, put in the cucumber with the remaining butter cut in small pieces. Mix in the chives and season well with salt and freshly ground black pepper.

Cover and cook in a moderate oven (180°C, 350°F, Gas Mark 4) for about 30 minutes or until tender. If you are using a flameproof casserole you can put it on a low heat on top of the cooker. Courgettes and young marrow can be cooked in the same way but should be sliced a little thinner.

Seakale
with cream and chives

METRIC/IMPERIAL/AMERICAN
450g/1lb/1lb seakale
1 tablespoon lemon juice
1 litre/2 pints/2½ pints boiling salted water

175ml/6fl oz/¾ cup single cream
1 tablespoon snipped chives
salt and pepper to taste

Cut the roots off the seakale and wash carefully. Add the lemon juice to a shallow pan of boiling salted water and simmer the seakale very gently for 20 minutes or until tender. Drain well. Heat the cream in the warm saucepan and add the chives. Put in the drained seakale carefully so that the tops are all lying in the same direction. Heat through without boiling. Arrange the seakale on a warm serving dish, adjust the seasoning of the cream and pour over the seakale. This is delicious with fish or chicken.
Note: Salsify can be cooked in the same way but should first be blanched in boiling water and skinned. It will require longer cooking.

Chicken and chive dip

METRIC/IMPERIAL/AMERICAN
175g/6oz/¾ cup cooked chicken, finely minced
75g/3oz/3oz button mushrooms, finely chopped
2 tablespoons/2 tablespoons/3 tablespoons ground almonds
4 tablespoons/4 tablespoons/⅓ cup mayonnaise

4 tablespoons/4 tablespoons/⅓ cup soured cream
1 tablespoon snipped chives
salt and black pepper to taste
Garnish:
paprika or finely chopped parsley

Mix together the chicken, mushrooms and ground almonds. Blend together the mayonnaise, soured cream and chives. Season to taste with salt and freshly ground black pepper, add to the chicken mixture and chill until required.

To serve, put the dip into a bowl on a small tray and arrange round it little dishes containing savoury biscuits, potato crisps and raw vegetable nibbles — fresh radishes, little sticks of celery heart, tiny button mushrooms, cauliflower flowerets on cocktail sticks and young carrots cut into sticks like crinkle chips. Garnish the dip with paprika or finely chopped parsley.

Left: *Cider-baked onions (see page 124)*

Below: *Minted pea and cucumber soup*
(see page 114)

CORIANDER

The fresh leaves of this plant are used almost exclusively in curries and chutneys, but the spicy orange tang of the ripe seeds enhances a wide variety of savoury and sweet dishes. They can be used whole in slow-cooking dishes, but otherwise they should be crushed before use. They give an attractive flavour to pâtés, terrines, meat and game dishes and Mediterranean vegetables. They have a special affinity with cooked apples and pears, whether in savoury casseroles or sweet pies and compotes.

Leeks à la grecque

Illustrated on pages 88–9

METRIC/IMPERIAL/AMERICAN
600ml/1 pint/2½ cups stock or bouillon
150ml/¼ pint/⅔ cup olive oil
juice of 1 lemon
1 small stick celery
bouquet garni

10 peppercorns
12 coriander seeds
6 small leeks
salt to taste

Simmer the stock with the olive oil, lemon juice, celery, bouquet garni, peppercorns and coriander seeds for 5 minutes. Meanwhile, cut the green part and the root off the leeks and wash thoroughly. Put into the simmering stock, add salt to taste, cover and cook gently for 20 minutes or until tender.

Leave the leeks to cool in the liquid. When cold, arrange on an hors d'oeuvre or glass dish, reduce the liquid by boiling, cool and spoon a little over the leeks. Serve well chilled as an hors d'oeuvre or salad. Celery, mushrooms, baby courgettes and globe artichoke hearts are also excellent cooked in this way.

Chilled ratatouille

METRIC/IMPERIAL/AMERICAN
1 large or 2 small aubergines
2 courgettes
salt
2 medium onions
2 red or green peppers
3–4 tomatoes or 1 medium can tomatoes
1 clove garlic
3–4 tablespoons/3–4 tablespoons/4–5
    tablespoons olive oil

12 coriander seeds, crushed
1 teaspoon dried basil or
    2 teaspoons fresh basil
freshly ground pepper
lemon juice to taste
Garnish:
finely chopped parsley

Wash the aubergines and courgettes, remove the stalks but do not peel. Cut into slices. Spread on a cloth, sprinkle with salt and leave until excess moisture is exuded. Peel and slice the onions thinly. Cut the peppers in half, remove the stalk and seeds. Slice in thin strips. Skin the tomatoes and chop coarsely. Skin and chop garlic, or force through a press when required.

Heat the oil and fry the onions gently until transparent. Rinse the aubergines and courgettes, drain and add with the garlic and pepper strips. Cover and cook gently for 30–40 minutes, stirring occasionally. Add the tomatoes, coriander, basil, freshly ground black pepper and salt to taste. Chill thoroughly. Serve in individual hors d'oeuvre dishes and garnish with chopped parsley. Alternatively, serve as a salad with cold fish or meat.

Note: If you plan to freeze the ratatouille, do not add garlic until it is defrosted.

Koftas curry

(Spiced meat balls)

METRIC/IMPERIAL/AMERICAN
3 slices bread
2 small eggs
450g/1lb/1lb minced beef or lamb
1 teaspoon crushed coriander seeds
1 teaspoon ground cinnamon
1 teaspoon grated green ginger or
    finely chopped preserved ginger
pinch ground cloves

1 teaspoon finely chopped onion
1 clove garlic, pressed
salt
lemon juice to taste
beaten egg and breadcrumbs for frying
curry sauce
Garnish:
fresh coriander leaves

Cut the crusts off the bread, soak in beaten egg and crush with a fork. Break up the minced meat with a fork and mix in the crushed coriander seeds, cinnamon, ginger, ground cloves, onion and garlic. Season well with salt and sharpen to taste with lemon juice. Mix thoroughly and blend with the bread and egg mixture. Roll the meat into a sausage shape on a floured board. Divide into 8–10 equal portions and with floured fingers shape into balls. Coat in egg and breadcrumbs.

Heat deep fat to frying temperature — a cube of bread dropped in will rise to the top and crisp in 1 minute. Put the meat balls in a frying basket, not too many at a time, and fry until brown and crisp. Drain on soft kitchen paper. Arrange a border of fluffy boiled rice round a shallow casserole dish. Pile the meat balls in the centre and pour over a curry sauce. Garnish with fresh coriander leaves and serve with green coriander relish below.

Green coriander relish

METRIC/IMPERIAL/AMERICAN
100g/4oz/4oz fresh coconut or desiccated coconut
2 green chilli peppers
good handful fresh coriander leaves

1 tablespoon chopped onion
salt
lemon juice to taste

Grate the fresh coconut finely or soak the desiccated coconut in just enough hot water to cover, until softened. Drain well. Slit the chilli peppers and remove all the seeds carefully. Chop the chilli finely and the coriander leaves. Pound the chillies, onion and leaves in a mortar, or put into the liquidizer. Gradually add the coconut, pounding or blending until a smooth paste is obtained. Season with salt and sharpen to taste with lemon juice. Serve with curry or as a relish with cold meat.

CUMIN

The ripe seeds of this plant have a very spicy, slightly aniseed flavour which is popular in the highly spiced dishes of Spanish America and in Indian curries and chutneys.

Mexican beef stew

METRIC/IMPERIAL/AMERICAN
450g/1lb/1lb stewing beef
2 tablespoons/2 tablespoons/3 tablespoons vegetable oil
1 large onion, sliced
1 (396-g/14-oz/14-oz) can peeled tomatoes
1 (396-g/14-oz/14-oz) can red kidney beans

1 large green or red pepper
stock as required
1–2 teaspoons cumin seeds
$\frac{1}{4}$ teaspoon chilli powder
salt to taste

Cut the beef into neat pieces, removing fat and gristle. Heat the oil and fry the meat briskly until browned. Add the onion and cook gently until transparent. Add the tomatoes with their juice and the kidney beans. Remove the stalk and seeds from the pepper, chop and add to pan. Pour in sufficient stock to cover the meat and beans. Stir in the cumin seeds, chilli powder and salt to taste.

Cover and cook gently on the top of the cooker or in a moderate oven (160°C, 325°F, Gas Mark 3) for 1½ hours or until the meat is tender. A favourite Mexican garnish is finely shredded lettuce heart which looks and tastes good.

Above: *Guinea chick with cream,
rosemary and brandy sauce (see page 117)*

Left: *Breton beef casserole (see page 117)*

Lentil or haricot bean salad

METRIC/IMPERIAL/AMERICAN
100g/4oz/½ cup brown lentils or haricot beans
salt and black pepper to taste
3 tablespoons/3 tablespoons/¼ cup olive oil
2–3 tablespoons/2–3 tablespoons/3–4 tablespoons lemon juice
2 ripe tomatoes
4 large black olives
2 spring onions
1 clove garlic, pressed
1 teaspoon cumin seeds
Garnish:
1 tablespoon chopped mint

Soak the lentils or beans overnight and simmer until tender, adding the salt after they begin to soften. Drain. It is best to mix in the other ingredients while still hot so they absorb the flavours better. Mix the olive oil and about 2 tablespoons lemon juice together and stir into the lentils or beans. Skin and chop the tomatoes and add. Halve and stone the olives. Chop half and add, reserve the remainder for garnish. Chop and add the white part of the spring onions; chop and reserve the green part for garnish. Press and add the garlic and cumin seeds. Mix well, taste and adjust seasoning with salt, pepper and lemon juice. Allow to marinate and chill well before serving. Garnish with the chopped spring onion, chopped mint and black olives. Optional extras are anchovy fillets and hard-boiled egg — the white chopped and the yolk sieved. This makes an excellent hors d'oeuvre.

CURRY PLANT

The leaves of this plant have a strong aroma of curry and can be used fresh, dried or frozen and give a pleasant mild curry flavour to egg and chicken dishes when cooked.

Curry-stuffed eggs

METRIC/IMPERIAL/AMERICAN
4–6 hard-boiled eggs
2 tablespoons/2 tablespoons/3 tablespoons flaked canned salmon, sardines or tuna
2 teaspoons finely chopped curry plant leaves
2–3 tablespoons/2–3 tablespoons/3–4 tablespoons mayonnaise
lemon juice to taste
salt and pepper
Garnish:
garden cress
paprika
radishes

Shell the eggs, cut in half and then cut a piece off each half to make a flat base. Carefully scoop out the yolks and press through a sieve with a wooden spoon. Crush the flaked fish finely and mix with sieved yolk and finely chopped curry plant leaves. Add sufficient mayonnaise to bind the mixture into the consistency of thick cream. Season to taste with lemon juice, salt and freshly ground pepper. Snip some heads off the garden cress and line the hollows in the egg white cups. Put the stuffing in a piping bag and pipe it neatly into the eggs. Cap with the small pieces of egg white cut off from the base. Sprinkle the caps with paprika and garnish the dish with the remaining cress and radishes.

Curry chicken croquettes

METRIC/IMPERIAL/AMERICAN
25g/1oz/2 tablespoons butter or margarine
1 tablespoon finely chopped onion
2–3 teaspoons finely chopped curry plant leaves
25g/1oz/¼ cup flour
150ml/¼ pint/⅔ cup chicken stock or milk
1 tablespoon finely chopped parsley
salt and pepper
lemon juice to taste
275g/10oz/1¼ cups cooked chicken, minced
beaten egg and breadcrumbs for coating
vegetable oil or fat for deep frying
Garnish:
fried parsley sprigs

Melt the butter and fry the chopped onion and curry plant leaves until the onion is transparent. Remove from the heat and stir in the flour. Gradually blend in the stock or milk. Return to the heat, bring to the boil and simmer gently, stirring constantly, for 3–4 minutes. Add the parsley and season to taste with salt and pepper and lemon juice. Add sufficient sauce to the chicken to bind it into a thick mixture. Taste and adjust the seasoning. Spread in a dish to chill and stiffen.

When the mixture is cold, divide into equal portions and on a floured board, roll into cork shapes. Coat in egg and breadcrumbs twice and chill again. Half fill a deep pan with vegetable oil or fat and heat to 190°C/375°F, or you can test with a cube of bread which should rise and crisp in a minute. Lay the croquettes in a frying basket, not too many at a time, lower carefully into the hot oil or fat until covered and fry until golden brown. Drain on soft kitchen paper and keep warm. Fry the parsley sprigs until crisp but still bright green — remove from the oil or fat as soon as they stop sizzling. Arrange the croquettes on a hot serving platter and garnish with the fried parsley.

Coconut chutney

METRIC/IMPERIAL/AMERICAN
4 tablespoons/4 tablespoons/⅓ cup finely grated fresh coconut or desiccated coconut
2 green chilli peppers or ¼ teaspoon chilli powder

salt to taste
1 tablespoon groundnut oil
½ teaspoon mustard seeds
1 teaspoon chopped curry leaves
150ml/¼ pint/⅔ cup natural yogurt

If you are using desiccated coconut, soften it for 20 minutes in hot water and drain well before using. Slit the chillies, discard the seeds, chop finely and pound with the coconut and salt in a mortar or blend in a liquidizer.

Heat the oil in a frying pan and fry the mustard seeds and curry leaves until the seeds begin to pop. Add the coconut mixture and stir over a gentle heat for 2–3 minutes. Remove from the heat and, when cool, mix in the yogurt. Adjust the seasoning and serve with a curry. This is a fresh relish and will not keep like cooked chutneys.

The seeds have an aniseed flavour and are used in pickles, especially with cucumber and gherkin, but also in biscuits and cakes, like caraway seeds. The pretty feathery leaves and yellow flowers make a very attractive garnish. The leaves have a milder flavour than the seeds and are often used in fish dishes, Scandinavian open sandwiches, in sauces and to flavour dill vinegar.

DILL

Smoked mackerel pâté

METRIC/IMPERIAL/AMERICAN
350g/12oz/12oz smoked mackerel
50g/2oz/¼ cup butter, softened
150ml/¼ pint/⅔ cup soured cream
1 tablespoon snipped dill leaves
freshly ground black pepper

salt
lemon juice to taste
Garnish:
paprika
fresh dill leaves

Skin and bone the mackerel carefully and mash the flesh with a fork or in the liquidizer. Cream the butter and add the mackerel, mixing well. Blend in half the soured cream and the snipped dill. Season to taste with black pepper, salt and lemon juice. Turn the mixture into a small terrine or soufflé dish, smooth the top and spread over the remaining soured cream. Chill until required. Garnish with paprika and the tips of fresh dill leaves. Serve with crusty French bread or hot, thin brown toast.

Left: *Baked pork chops with apple and sage stuffing (see page 119)*

Below: *Chicory and orange salad with tarragon cream dressing (see page 123)*

Grilled salmon steaks

with dill cream sauce
Illustrated on page 92

METRIC/IMPERIAL/AMERICAN
4 fresh salmon steaks
salt and freshly ground black pepper
lemon juice to taste
50g/2oz/$\frac{1}{4}$ cup softened butter

Garnish:
lemon wedges
fresh dill leaves

Wash the salmon steaks to remove any blood. Dry on soft kitchen paper. Season with the salt, pepper and lemon juice. Place on the grill rack and dot with butter. Preheat the grill and cook the steaks for 8–10 minutes according to thickness. Turn the steaks over and season. Dot with butter and grill the second side until the flesh shrinks from the backbone.

Place the salmon steaks on a warmed serving plate and garnish with lemon wedges and dill. Serve with dill cream sauce or cucumber and dill sauce. If liked, accompany with buttered garlic spinach or casseroled cucumber with chives (see page 94).

Dill cream sauce

METRIC/IMPERIAL/AMERICAN
40g/1$\frac{1}{2}$oz/3 tablespoons butter
1 tablespoon finely chopped onion
40g/1$\frac{1}{2}$oz/6 tablespoons flour
300ml/$\frac{1}{2}$ pint/1$\frac{1}{4}$ cups fish stock or milk
2 tablespoons/2 tablespoons/3 tablespoons
  snipped fresh dill or 1–2 teaspoons
  dill seeds

4 tablespoons/4 tablespoons/$\frac{1}{3}$ cup
  soured cream
salt and freshly ground pepper

Melt the butter and fry the onion until transparent. Remove from the heat and stir in the flour. Blend in the fish stock or milk. Return to the heat, bring to the boil, add the snipped dill and simmer for 3–4 minutes, stirring steadily. Stir in the soured cream and season well with salt and freshly ground pepper.

If soured cream is not available, use double cream and stir in 1 tablespoon of lemon juice.

Cucumber and dill sauce

Follow the recipe for dill cream sauce but replace the chopped onion with half a cucumber, peeled and diced, and use fish or chicken stock instead of milk which the cucumber tends to curdle.

ELDER

The flowers have a delicate honeyed muscatel flavour when in full bloom and make delightful sweet fritters. They can be added during cooking to various fruit preserves, but seem to have a special affinity with gooseberries. The ripe berries have a sharper flavour and can be added to muffins and doughnuts. They are often made into home-made wines.

Elder flower fritters

METRIC/IMPERIAL/AMERICAN
100g/4oz/1 cup flour
pinch salt
1 egg, separated
175ml/6fl oz/$\frac{3}{4}$ cup warm water

12 elder flower heads
oil or fat for deep frying
vanilla or cinnamon sugar for dredging

Sift the flour and salt into a bowl. Make a well in the centre and drop in the egg yolk. Add a little water and stir the flour in gradually, drawing it in from the sides of the well.

Trim the stalks of the elder flower heads. Just before frying, whisk the egg white until stiff, but still moist, and fold into the batter. Heat the deep oil or fat until a cube of bread when dropped in will rise to the surface and crisp in one minute.

Hold the flower head by the stalk, dip into the batter, allow the surplus to drain back into the bowl and fry the fritter until golden and crisp. Drain on soft kitchen paper, sprinkle with castor sugar flavoured with a vanilla bean or ground cinnamon and serve immediately.

Elder and gooseberry jelly

METRIC/IMPERIAL/AMERICAN
1·75kg/4lb/4lb green gooseberries
600ml–1 litre/1–2 pints/2½–5 cups water

granulated sugar
4–8 elder flower heads according to size

Cover the gooseberries with water, no need to top and tail, then simmer uncovered for about 2 hours. Strain through a jelly bag, preferably overnight.

To each 600ml/1 pint/2½ cups of juice add 450g/1lb/1lb warmed sugar and heat gently until the sugar is dissolved. Tie the elder flowers in a muslin bag and add to the syrup. Heat to boiling point and boil briskly for 10 minutes until setting point is reached. Remove the elder flowers, pot the jelly and cover.

METRIC/IMPERIAL/AMERICAN
1·5kg/3lb/3lb green gooseberries
300ml/½ pint/1¼ cups water

1·25kg/2½lb/2½lb sugar
9 elder flower heads

Elder and gooseberry syrup

Top, tail and wash the gooseberries. Put them in a pan with the water and simmer gently until soft but still whole. Add the sugar and dissolve over gentle heat. Wash the elder flower heads but leave on stalks. Tie the elder flowers in a muslin bag, add and simmer gently about 8–10 minutes until the syrup is well flavoured. Remove the flower heads and strain the gooseberries through muslin. Pour the syrup into bottles or preserving jars and seal well.

Sterilize by putting in a deep pan or sterilizer. Cover with cold water. Heat slowly taking an hour to reach simmering point. Keep simmering very gently for 20–30 minutes according to the size of the bottles or jars. Remove from the pan, cool, label and store. The elder flowers give this syrup a delicate muscatel flavour which is delicious added to fruit salads and compotes. The gooseberries left from making the syrup can be used for gooseberry purée and fool.

Elderberry and apple jelly

METRIC/IMPERIAL/AMERICAN
1·5kg/3lb/3lb cooking apples or windfalls
2·25 litres/4 pints/5 pints elderberries, stalked

sugar
piece orange peel
½ stick cinnamon

Wash the apples, cut into pieces, removing any blemishes. Put into a pan with the washed elderberries and just cover with cold water. Bring to the boil and simmer until a pulp. Strain through a jelly bag, leaving to drip overnight. Measure the juice and add 450g/1lb/1lb sugar for each 600ml/1 pint/2½ cups. Stir over a gentle heat until the sugar is dissolved, add the orange rind and cinnamon, tied together, and boil rapidly to setting point – test on a cold saucer, the jelly will wrinkle when pushed if ready. Remove the orange rind and cinnamon; pot, label and seal.

Herb butters (see page 126)

FENNEL

The seeds and leaves of this plant have a distinctive aniseed flavour, but the aroma of the leaves is volatile so they are used in rather generous quantities. The seeds are more potent and 1–2 teaspoons in a sauce or stuffing recipe is usually sufficient. Fennel flavour goes particularly well with oily fish like salmon, mackerel, herring and pilchards and with rich meat like pork.

Baked mackerel
with mushroom and fennel stuffing

METRIC/IMPERIAL/AMERICAN
4 fresh mackerel
vegetable oil for baking
100ml/4fl oz/½ cup cider or white wine
8 mushroom caps
4 tomatoes
2 tablespoons/2 tablespoons/3 tablespoons melted butter
Stuffing:
100g/4oz/4oz mushrooms, chopped
1 tablespoon chopped onion

40g/1½oz/3 tablespoons butter or margarine
75g/3oz/generous ½ cup rice, cooked
2 tablespoons/2 tablespoons/3 tablespoons chopped fresh fennel leaves
grated rind and juice of 1 lemon
salt and freshly ground pepper to taste
Garnish:
fresh fennel leaves
lemon wedges

Clean the mackerel and trim the tails neatly. Remove the heads if preferred.
To prepare the stuffing, fry the chopped mushrooms and onion in the butter until the onion is transparent. Mix in the rice, chopped fennel leaves, grated lemon rind and juice. Season to taste with salt and freshly ground black pepper. Spoon into the mackerel and sew up the opening, or secure with small poultry skewers or wooden cocktail sticks (plastic ones will melt in cooking).

Grease a baking tin, put in the stuffed mackerel and brush with oil. Pour in the cider or wine. Lay a sheet of greased kitchen foil on top – do not tuck it in tightly or the fish will steam instead of bake.

Bake in centre of a moderately hot oven (200°C, 400°F, Gas Mark 6) for 30 minutes. Remove the foil, add the mushroom caps, black side uppermost, and tomatoes cut in half. Pour the melted butter over the vegetables and fish and season with salt and pepper. Return to the oven without the foil for a further 10–15 minutes to finish cooking. Serve the mackerel garnished with fresh fennel leaves and lemon wedges.
Note: Fresh herring may be used instead of mackerel and the baking time adjusted to the size of the fish.

Flamed red mullet
with fennel

METRIC/IMPERIAL/AMERICAN
4 red mullet
lemon juice to taste
salt and freshly ground black pepper
50g/2oz/¼ cup butter, melted
dried fennel stalks

2 tablespoons/2 tablespoons/3 tablespoons brandy
Garnish:
lemon wedges
fresh fennel leaves

This famous provençale dish is good to eat and fun to cook. You can use grey mullet, but it is not so tasty, or mackerel. Bass and sea bream are also excellent, but as they are large you will need only one good sized fish and it should be baked, not grilled. Clean the red mullet, but leave the liver inside. Rub the inside of the fish with lemon juice and season with salt and freshly ground black pepper. Make 3 slits on each side and season with salt, pepper and lemon juice. Place on a greased grid in a grilling pan or in a roasting tin if you are going to bake it.

Pour over the melted butter and grill for about 10 minutes on each side or bake in a moderately hot oven (190°C, 375°F, Gas Mark 5) until the flesh shrinks away from backbone, at the thick end. When grilling, baste liberally with melted butter when you carefully turn the fish over.

Spread the dried fennel, about 3·5cm/1½ inches deep, over the base of a flameproof dish or shallow casserole and place the grid with the cooked fish over the fennel. Warm the brandy in a ladle or small saucepan, ignite it and pour over the fish. The fennel will catch alight and the scent gives the fish a special flavour. This can be done on a side table in the dining room when entertaining your guests. When the flames die down, serve the fish on warm plates, garnished with fresh lemon wedges and fennel leaves. Serve with boiled new potatoes with plenty of melted butter.

GARLIC

This is the member of the onion family which not only has the most potent flavour, but also the most persistent. Some people only like it when it is introduced into a dish with discretion, so there is just a whisper of its aroma, others revel in the robust flavour of the Mediterranean dishes where it greets you with a 'wham'. This could be distressful to some of your guests so you must choose carefully. If you want a mild flavour, crush the skinned garlic clove in a press, use only the juice and discard the rest. For a stronger flavour, chop it finely, crush with a knife and add it to a sauce, casserole or pâté. Whole cloves can be inserted into joints for roasting and garlic butter is used for grills.

For a whiff in a salad, put a 'chapon' in the bottom of the bowl — this is a slice of French bread well-flavoured with garlic. It will 'perfume' the salad vegetables and one of the garlic addicts will no doubt eat the 'chapon' with pleasure. Alternatively, use garlic-flavoured oil or vinegar or garlic salt in the dressing. Fresh dry bulbs keep very well, but do not cook garlic in dishes you intend to freeze because it goes very peppery. Add it after defrosting. Take care to cover closely any garlic-flavoured dishes you put in the refrigerator, a bowl of delicious Tuscan beans (see page 119) can ruin the milk and cream in no time.

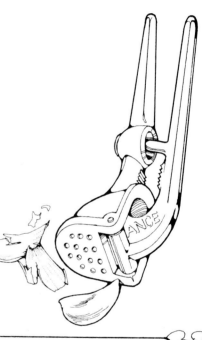

Provençale fish soup

Illustrated on page 93

METRIC/IMPERIAL/AMERICAN

1 large onion, sliced	bouquet garni, including fennel
2 leeks	1kg/2lb/2lb whiting or other white fish
1 carrot, diced	1·5litres/2½ pints/3 pints water
4 tablespoons/4 tablespoons/⅓ cup olive oil	good pinch saffron
	2 teaspoons salt
4 ripe tomatoes, chopped, or 1 small can peeled tomatoes	freshly ground pepper
	1 tablespoon chopped parsley
2 cloves garlic, crushed	50g/2oz/½ cup cut macaroni

Fry the onion, chopped white part of the leeks and carrot gently in the olive oil until softened, but not coloured. Add the tomatoes, garlic, herbs and the fish, cut into pieces but not boned. Simmer for 10 minutes, stirring well. Add the water, saffron, salt and freshly ground pepper. Cook for 20 minutes then press through a sieve. Pour the soup back into the saucepan, bring to the boil, add the parsley and macaroni and simmer for 10–15 minutes until the macaroni is cooked. Taste and season well. Serve very hot with grated Parmesan or Gruyère cheese handed separately or stirred into the soup just before serving. Accompany with hot garlic bread.

Alternatively, spread slices of French bread with garlic butter and bake until crisp. Put a baked croûte in each soup bowl and pour the soup on top.

111

Garlic bread

METRIC/IMPERIAL/AMERICAN
1 short French loaf
2–3 cloves garlic
75g/3oz/6 tablespoons softened butter

Warm the loaf in the oven. Chop and crush the garlic cloves with a knife or put through the garlic press. Beat into the softened butter. Cut the warm bread down in thick slices, but not quite through to the bottom of the loaf. Spread each slice with garlic butter. Reform the loaf, wrap in foil and place in a preheated hot oven (220°C, 425°F, Gas Mark 7) for 10–15 minutes and serve hot.

Baked mushrooms
with garlic butter

METRIC/IMPERIAL/AMERICAN
450g/1lb/1lb mushrooms
salt and freshly ground pepper
grated rind and juice of 1 small lemon
175g/6oz/¾ cup garlic butter (see page 126)

4 tablespoons/4 tablespoons/⅓ cup dry breadcrumbs
Garnish:
chopped parsley

Remove the stalks, wash the mushroom caps and arrange them, dark side uppermost in 4 well-buttered gratin dishes. Season with salt, pepper and lemon juice. Cream the garlic butter with the lemon rind and work in the breadcrumbs. Shape into a roll and chill.

Cover the mushrooms with foil and bake in a moderately hot oven (200°C, 400°F, Gas Mark 6) for 15 minutes until partly cooked only. Cut the garlic butter rolls into slices and put one on each mushroom cap. Return to the oven until crispy or finish under the grill. Garnish with chopped fresh parsley.

Serve as a first course with crusty French bread (to mop up the garlic butter, French style) or bake in one large dish and serve with grilled fish or meat.

MARJORAM

The flavour of marjoram is sweet, rather like thyme, and varies in strength according to species. The pot marjoram is popular both for growing and cooking. In hot sunshine, marjoram develops a strong aroma which can be too potent if used overgenerously. The flavour blends very well with vegetables of the cabbage family and tomatoes, and is used to season many stuffings and terrines.

Partridge or wood pigeon
with cabbage and red wine
Illustrated opposite

METRIC/IMPERIAL/AMERICAN
2 partridge or 4 wood pigeon
2 or 4 small sprigs marjoram
4 rashers streaky bacon
2 tablespoons/2 tablespoons/3 tablespoons seasoned flour
50g/2oz/¼ cup dripping or lard
1 large onion, sliced
100g/4oz/4oz pickled pork, chopped

1 small cabbage, white or green
salt and freshly ground pepper
1 teaspoon dried marjoram
100ml/4fl oz/½ cup red wine
4 frankfurter sausages
Garnish:
watercress sprigs

Clean the birds and put a sprig of fresh marjoram in each. Remove any rind and gristle from the bacon, cover the breasts of the birds and truss neatly. Sprinkle with seasoned flour.

Heat the fat in a deep flameproof casserole and fry the onion gently until softened. Add the chopped pork and the birds and brown all over. Remove the birds from the casserole. Shred finely and wash 450g/1lb/1lb cabbage, discarding the stalk. If using green cabbage, blanch for 5 minutes in boiling salted water and drain. Put a thick layer of cabbage in the bottom of the casserole, mixing it with the onion and pickled pork. Season with salt and freshly ground pepper and sprinkle with dried marjoram. Put the birds on top. Cover with the remaining cabbage. Pour

Partridge or wood pigeon with cabbage and red wine

over the red wine and season again. Put a lid on the casserole and cook over a gentle heat on top of the cooker or in a moderate oven (180°C, 350°F, Gas Mark 4) for 1 hour. Add frankfurter sausages and continue cooking for another hour or until tender. If the liquid evaporates too much, add extra water or stock. Serve in the casserole or arrange the birds on a warm platter surrounded by the cabbage and sausages. Garnish with watercress.

Note: Older partridge can be used for this dish and it is a tasty way of cooking frozen birds.

Pork and mushroom terrine

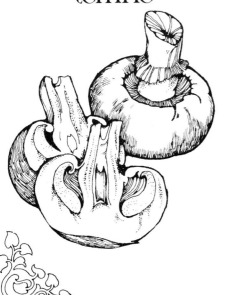

METRIC/IMPERIAL/AMERICAN
225g/8oz/1 cup lean pork, minced
225g/8oz/1 cup veal or beef, minced
4 button onions, finely chopped
1 teaspoon dried marjoram
1 tablespoon finely chopped fresh parsley
1 clove garlic, pressed
salt and ground pepper to taste
2 eggs, beaten

100g/4oz/4oz button mushrooms
50g/2oz/½ cup Gouda cheese, diced
1 thick slice cooked ham, diced
cranberry or redcurrant jelly
Garnish:
thin slices of lemon
1–2 fresh bay leaves

Mix the pork with the veal or beef, onions, marjoram and parsley. Add the juice from the pressed garlic and season generously with salt and freshly ground pepper. Stir in the beaten eggs.

Grease a 1-litre/2-pint/2½-pint terrine and press in half the meat mixture. Slice the mushrooms. Mix with the diced cheese and ham and spread this filling over the minced meat and cover with remaining meat mixture. Arrange the sliced lemon and bay leaves on top. Cover with a buttered piece of greaseproof paper and put the lid on the terrine or cover with foil. Place the terrine in a roasting tin with 1 cm/½ inch of water in the bottom and put in the centre of a moderate oven (180°C, 350°F, Gas Mark 4) and cook for 1½ hours. The terrine is cooked when the juice which rises to the top is no.longer pink.

Remove from the oven. Take off the greaseproof paper and glaze the top with hot cranberry or redcurrant jelly.

Serve cold with crusty French bread and butter as a first course or with green and potato salads for a lunch or supper dish.

MINT

This is a favourite herb in English, Mediterranean and Middle Eastern cookery, especially the spearmint and apple mint varieties which have a refreshing sharp taste. The fresh leaves are used to flavour soups, sauces and stuffings, especially for lamb; to garnish fresh vegetables and salads, cold sorbets and drinks. The crystallized leaves make an attractive decoration for cakes and cold desserts. Dried mint loses colour but retains its flavour fairly well and is very useful in winter for sauces and stuffings. It is better frozen.

Minted pea and cucumber soup

Illustrated on page 97

METRIC/IMPERIAL/AMERICAN
1 large onion
2 rashers bacon or ham trimmings
1 small lettuce
50g/2oz/¼ cup butter
225g/8oz/1½ cups shelled peas or
    1 small can green peas
2 tablespoons/2 tablespoons/3 tablespoons
    flour
300ml/½ pint/1¼ cups milk

1 tablespoon chopped fresh mint
300ml/½ pint/1¼ cups white stock or
    water
1 cucumber
salt
lemon juice to taste
Garnish:
cream
chopped fresh mint or mint sprigs

Peel and slice the onion. Chop the bacon, discarding any rind and gristle. Shred and wash lettuce, drain in a colander.

Melt the butter and fry the onion and bacon until the onion is transparent. Add the shredded lettuce, cover and sweat over low heat for a few minutes until bright green and juicy. Add the peas (if using canned, drain and reserve liquor). Blend in sufficient flour to absorb the fat, stir in the milk and bring to the simmer (add the liquor from the canned peas). Stirring steadily, add the mint and thin as required with the stock or water. Grate the unpeeled cucumber and add. (If serving the soup cold, reserve half the cucumber.) Salt to taste, cover and simmer gently for about 45 minutes. Put through mouli or sieve. Adjust the seasoning with salt and lemon juice.

To garnish, add 2–3 tablespoons/2–3 tablespoons/3–4 tablespoons cream, fresh or soured and sprinkle with chopped fresh mint.

To serve cold, after sieving the soup, peel and grate in remaining half cucumber. Season well with salt and lemon juice and chill thoroughly. Pour into soup bowls, add a swirl of cream in the centre and a small mint sprig. For a party, stand each soup cup in a small bowl, surround with crushed ice garnished with fresh mint leaves – it is attractive and delicious.

Lamb guard of honour

METRIC/IMPERIAL/AMERICAN
1 pair best ends of lamb
pineapple and mint stuffing (see page 125),
    using 1 (439-g/15½-oz/15½-oz) can
    pineapple rings

oil for roasting
Garnish:
mint sprigs

Ask the butcher to remove the chine bone from 2 matching best ends with 6 cutlets on each. Remove a strip of meat 2·5cm/1 inch wide from the ends of the cutlet so the bones protrude. Scrape them clean. With a sharp knife, mark the fat on the outside of the joints into diamonds.

Stand the joints facing each other with the bones interlocking like the swords of a guard of honour. Make the stuffing (see page 125), using 4 rings of canned pineapple. Fill the cavity between the joints. Put a piece of foil at each end and secure the joint with skewers and string. Stand it in a greased roasting tin and brush with oil.

Roast in a moderate oven (190°C, 375°F, Gas Mark 5) for 1½ hours or until the juice runs out amber colour when tested with a skewer. Remove the joint to a warm serving plate. Fry the remaining pineapple rings in the fat in the roasting tin, and arrange round meat. Pour off the fat carefully, leaving the residue in tin and add the pineapple juice. Boil briskly scraping up residue, season well and strain into warm gravy boat. Just before serving, remove the string and skewers from the joint, garnish with sprigs of fresh mint.

This is the most widely used of all the herbs for garnishing, flavouring and sometimes for colouring food. It is almost too popular for garnishing, but one of its advantages is that its sprigs of bright green curly leaves do not wilt quickly, even on hot food, and chopped it adds both colour and flavour to all kinds of dishes. The stalks have more flavour than the leaves and are used in a 'bouquet garni' with thyme and bay leaf, for meat and fish stocks and marinades. It is also always included in the 'fines herbes' mixture. Parsley loses flavour when dried, but both stalks and leaves freeze well and should be packed separately.

PARSLEY

Pork or veal rolls
with frittatas

METRIC/IMPERIAL/AMERICAN
8 small escalopes of pork or veal
seasoned flour
Frittatas:
2 large thin slices Mortadella sausage
   or lean cooked ham
2 eggs, beaten
2 tablespoons/2 tablespoons/3 tablespoons
   chopped fresh parsley
2 tablespoons/2 tablespoons/3 tablespoons
   grated Parmesan cheese
40g/1½oz/3 tablespoons butter
Mushroom sauce:
50g/2oz/¼ cup butter or margarine

1 medium onion, sliced
100–175g/4–6oz/4–6oz mushrooms,
   sliced
2 tablespoons/2 tablespoons/3 tablespoons
   flour
150ml/¼ pint/⅔ cup milk
salt and pepper
lemon juice to taste
150ml/¼ pint/⅔ cup stock
Garnish:
lemon slices
parsley sprigs

Beat out the meat thinly and trim neatly. To make the frittatas, dice the Mortadella or ham and add to the beaten eggs. Mix in the chopped parsley and Parmesan cheese.

Heat the butter in a frying pan and drop in the frittata mixture in spoonfuls so it spreads into little thin pancakes. Fry until golden brown underneath, turn and fry on the other side.

Cover each escalope with a frittata, trimming it to fit. Roll up like a little Swiss roll and secure with string. Roll in a seasoned flour and pat off any surplus.

For the sauce, heat the butter in a sauté pan and fry the meat rolls until golden brown all over. Remove from the pan, add the onion and fry gently until softened. Add the mushrooms and fry lightly. Remove from the heat and stir in sufficient flour to absorb the fat. Blend in the milk. Return to the heat, bring to the boil and simmer. Season with salt, pepper and lemon juice and put in the meat rolls. Add the stock until rolls are nearly covered. Cover and simmer gently until the meat is tender — about 45 minutes according to thickness of the rolls. Adjust the seasoning and serve garnished with fresh lemon slices and parsley sprigs.

Potatoes maître d'hôtel

METRIC/IMPERIAL/AMERICAN
550g/1¼lb/1¼lb potatoes
2 teaspoons salt
25g/1oz/2 tablespoons butter
freshly ground pepper

2 tablespoons/2 tablespoons/3 tablespoons
   chopped fresh parsley
1 tablespoon chopped chives or shallot
milk to cover

Scrub the potatoes and boil in their skins with the salt until cooked, but still firm. Drain and cover with a clean cloth to dry off. Peel and slice.

Melt the butter in a flameproof casserole and put in the sliced potatoes in layers, seasoning each layer with salt, freshly ground pepper and sprinkle with chopped parsley and chives or shallot. Heat about 300ml/½ pint/1¼ cups milk and pour over the potatoes to cover them. Heat through over a gentle heat — about 10 minutes. Serve from the casserole. These potatoes are very good with fish and chicken; for a richer dish, use single cream instead of milk.

Mustard turnips
with parsley

METRIC/IMPERIAL/AMERICAN
450g/1lb/1lb young white turnips
salt
50g/2oz/¼ cup unsalted butter
1–2 tablespoons/1–2 tablespoons/1–3
   tablespoons continental mustard

2 tablespoons/2 tablespoons/3 tablespoons
   chopped fresh parsley

Many people who say they do not like turnips eat them happily when prepared in this way.

Peel the turnips and cut into little sticks like potato chips. Drop into boiling salted water and simmer for 15–20 minutes until cooked, but still firm. Be careful not to overcook. Turn into a colander to drain and cover with a cloth to keep warm and dry. Soften the butter in a hot pan, it should be creamy, not oily. Blend in the mustard, up to 2 tablespoons if mild. Stir in the turnips gradually, making sure they are all coated and taking care not to break them. Just before serving, mix in the parsley and serve hot.

Breton beef casserole

Illustrated on page 100

METRIC/IMPERIAL/AMERICAN
100g/4oz/½ cup haricot beans
1 medium onion
5 cloves
0.75kg/1½lb/1½lb chuck steak
3 tablespoons/3 tablespoons/¼ cup seasoned flour
50g/2oz/¼ cup butter or margarine
225g/8oz/8oz button onions, peeled
2 sticks celery, chopped
1 clove garlic, chopped

100ml/4fl oz/½ cup dry cider or white wine
150ml/¼ pint/⅔ cup tomato juice
2 tablespoons/2 tablespoons/3 table- spoons chopped parsley
2 teaspoons chopped fresh lemon thyme or 1 teaspoon dried lemon thyme
1 teaspoon sugar
salt and freshly ground pepper to taste
225g/8oz/1½ cups carrots, sliced
100g/4oz/⅔ cup turnip, diced

Soak the haricot beans overnight. Drain and put in a saucepan with the onion spiked with the cloves, cover with fresh cold water (not salt as it hardens the beans) and simmer for 1½ hours or until beans are tender.

Cut the meat into 5-cm/2-inch cubes, removing any fat and gristle. Toss in a paper bag with the seasoned flour until well coated. Heat the butter or margarine in a flameproof casserole. Shake the loose flour off the meat and fry the meat briskly in the hot fat until nicely browned all over. Remove the meat, fry the onions until golden and remove from the casserole. Fry the celery and garlic, sprinkle on the remaining seasoned flour from the bag, and fry, stirring steadily, until caramel coloured.

Remove the casserole from the heat and blend in first the cider or wine and then the tomato juice. Stir until smooth, replace on the heat and bring to the boil. Add the meat and sufficient water to cover. Add 1 tablespoon parsley, 2 teaspoons fresh lemon thyme, sugar, salt and freshly ground pepper to taste. Cover and simmer over a gentle heat for 45 minutes. Add the onions, drained beans, carrots and turnip and continue simmering for 45 minutes to 1 hour until the meat is tender. Taste and adjust the seasoning. Garnish with remaining fresh parsley and serve with creamed potatoes.

Fresh rosemary is available all the year round and sprigs are often used for marinades and basting sauces, and spiked into roasting lamb. The leaves are spiky and fairly tough, so must be finely chopped, whether fresh, frozen or dried. They are very aromatic and particularly good with veal, pork, poultry and game, but should be used with discretion as some people find the flavour rather powerful. The flowers make a pretty, edible garnish.

ROSEMARY

Guinea chick
with cream, rosemary and brandy sauce (Serves 2)

Illustrated on page 101

METRIC/IMPERIAL/AMERICAN
1 guinea chick
1 sprig rosemary
1 bay leaf
1 chicken stock cube
50g/2oz/¼ cup butter
1 medium onion, chopped
100g/4oz/4oz button mushrooms
4 tablespoons/4 tablespoons/⅓ cup brandy

15g/½oz/1 tablespoon butter
2 teaspoons flour
150ml/¼ pint/⅔ cup cream
1 teaspoon finely chopped fresh rosemary or ½ teaspoon dried rosemary
Garnish:
lemon slices
rosemary sprigs

Cut the guinea chick in half down the backbone. Put the neck and cleaned giblets in a saucepan with the sprig of rosemary, bay leaf and 600ml/

1 pint/2½ cups water. Crumble in the stock cube, cover and simmer gently until required.

Heat the butter in a flameproof casserole and fry the onion and mushrooms gently until softened. Put in the bird and fry briskly until golden brown all over. Warm half the brandy in a small saucepan, set alight by tipping gently into the gas or other naked flame. Pour over the bird and shake well until the flames die down. Add the strained giblet stock, bring to the boil, cover and simmer gently on top of the cooker or in a moderate oven (160°C, 325°F, Gas Mark 3) for 45–60 minutes or until tender. Remove from the casserole.

Make kneaded butter by creaming together the butter and flour. Divide into little pieces and whisk into the cooking liquid. Cook gently until thickened. Mix the cream, remaining brandy and a little sauce and blend this back into the sauce in the casserole. Adjust the seasoning and add the finely chopped rosemary. Replace the bird, heat through without boiling and serve garnished with lemon slices and rosemary sprigs.

Jugged hare
with rosemary and juniper berries

METRIC/IMPERIAL/AMERICAN

1 young hare, skinned and paunched
salt and pepper
Marinade:
2 tablespoons/2 tablespoons/3 tablespoons olive oil
2 tablespoons/2 tablespoons/3 tablespoons wine vinegar
1 small onion, sliced
7 peppercorns
7 juniper berries, crushed
bouquet garni
1 sprig rosemary
1 teaspoon salt
Sauce:
50g/2oz/¼ cup butter or margarine
75g/3oz/scant ½ cup bacon or ham, chopped
2 medium onions, sliced
2 sticks celery, chopped
225g/8oz/8oz carrots, sliced
about 2 tablespoons/2 tablespoons/3 tablespoons flour
450ml/¾ pint/2 cups meat stock
freshly ground pepper
3 tablespoons/3 tablespoons/¼ cup redcurrant jelly
3 tablespoons/3 tablespoons/¼ cup port
3 tablespoons/3 tablespoons/¼ cup hare blood (optional)
1 teaspoon lemon juice
Garnish:
chopped parsley

Joint the hare into 8 pieces. Cut off the belly flaps and cook with the seasoning into stock with the liver, kidneys and heart. Keep any blood in a basin if to be used for sauce. Mix the ingredients for the marinade, put in the hare joints and leave for several hours, preferably overnight. Drain the joints and dry on soft kitchen paper.

Heat the butter in a deep flameproof casserole and fry the joints until they are slate-coloured all over, then remove.

Fry the bacon or ham, onion, celery and carrots until beginning to colour. Add sufficient flour to absorb the fat and fry, stirring well, until browning. Remove from the heat and blend in the marinade. Bring to a simmer, put in the hare joints and add sufficient stock to cover the hare; adjust the seasoning. Cover and cook very gently on top of the cooker or in a cool oven (150°C, 300°F, Gas Mark 2) for 2½–3 hours until tender.

Remove the rosemary sprig and bouquet garni and stir in the redcurrant jelly and port. Cook gently until the jelly is dissolved. If using hare blood, mix with the lemon juice and add. If not using blood, sharpen the sauce to taste with the lemon juice.

Deep fry stuffing balls (see page 125) and place on top of the jugged hare. Garnish with chopped fresh parsley. Serve with creamed potatoes and Brussels sprouts seasoned with nutmeg.

SAGE

This is a very useful herb as you can gather its leaves for most of the year, but they have such a strong aromatic flavour they have to be used with discretion as too much can easily spoil a dish. They are best used with robust-tasting sauces and stuffings, and pork and game dishes. They add flavour to winter vegetables and some cheeses. Flowers and leafy sprigs make an attractive garnish.

Baked pork chops
with apple and sage stuffing
Illustrated on page 104

METRIC/IMPERIAL/AMERICAN
4 neck or loin pork chops
50g/2oz/¼ cup lard or butter
100ml/4fl oz/½ cup dry cider or white wine
Stuffing:
2 slices bread
1 medium cooking apple
50g/2oz/¼ cup butter or margarine
1 tablespoon finely chopped onion
1 tablespoon finely chopped celery
2 tablespoons/2 tablespoons/3 tablespoons chopped salted peanuts
2 teaspoons finely chopped fresh sage or 1 teaspoon dried sage
freshly ground pepper
lemon juice to taste
Garnish:
fresh sage sprigs
watercress sprig

Trim most of the fat off the chops. Cut a large gash from the outside of each chop down to the bone to make a pocket.

For the stuffing, remove the crusts from the bread and cut into dice. Peel, core and dice the apple. Heat the butter in a small saucepan and fry the onion, celery and apple until softened. Add the nuts and the bread, and continue cooking and stirring until the apple is softened. Mix in the chopped sage and season with pepper and lemon juice.

Pack the stuffing into the pockets in the chops and secure with small skewers or wooden cocktail sticks. Seal the chops on both sides in hot fat in a shallow flameproof casserole or in a frying pan and when nicely browned, arrange in an ovenproof gratin dish. Add the cider or wine and bake in a moderate oven (180°C, 350°F, Gas Mark 4) for 45–50 minutes until tender. Remove the skewers or cocktail sticks and garnish with sprigs of fresh sage and watercress. Serve with potatoes baked in their jackets.
Note: Neck cutlets of veal can be stuffed and cooked in the same way.

Tuscan green beans

METRIC/IMPERIAL/AMERICAN
450g/1lb/1lb French beans
salt
50g/2oz/¼ cup butter
1 tablespoon olive oil
1 clove garlic, crushed
1 tablespoon chopped fresh sage or savory
pinch ground nutmeg
freshly ground pepper
1 tablespoon grated Parmesan cheese

Top and tail the beans and string if necessary. Simmer in boiling salted water until cooked but still crisp. Drain and cover with a cloth to keep warm.

Heat the butter and oil, stir in the garlic and 2 teaspoons of herbs; fry for 1 minute. Add the beans, nutmeg, salt and pepper to taste and, over gentle heat, turn carefully in the hot fat so as not to break them.

Mix in the grated Parmesan and serve at once, sprinkled with the remaining fresh herbs.

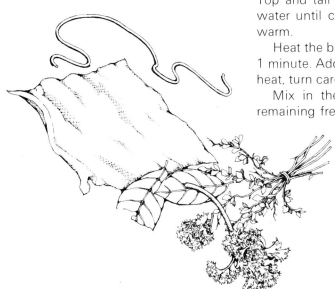

METRIC/IMPERIAL/AMERICAN
8 small veal escalopes
8 small slices cooked ham
fresh sage leaves
50g/2oz/¼ cup butter
3 tablespoons/3 tablespoons/¼ cup
  Marsala or sweet vermouth

150ml/¼ pint/⅔ cup white stock
salt and freshly ground black pepper
4 tablespoons/4 tablespoons/⅓ cup
  cream
Garnish:
sage leaves

Veal
escalopes
with ham and sage

Beat the veal escalopes until flat and thin. Trim the ham slices to the same size as the escalopes. Lay one on each escalope and put a fresh sage leaf on top. Roll up the escalopes neatly and tie with string.

Heat the butter and fry the rolls until nicely browned all over. Add the Marsala or vermouth and simmer for a few minutes. Add the stock and season to taste. Cover and cook gently on top of the cooker or in a moderate oven (160°C, 325°F, Gas Mark 3) for 15–20 minutes until tender. Place the rolls on a warm serving dish and remove the string. Reduce the sauce by boiling briskly if necessary. Mix 3 tablespoons/3 tablespoons/¼ cup of sauce with the cream, pour this back into the pan. Adjust the seasoning and pour over veal. Garnish with fresh sage leaves, chopped or in sprigs, and serve with pasta or fluffy boiled rice.

SAVORY

The leaves of both summer and winter savory have a piquant aromatic taste which many people prefer to sage in sauces and stuffings for pork, duck, goose and game casseroles. In France, it is often used to flavour green and broad beans and in salads made with cooked vegetables and dried haricot and butter beans. It retains its flavour when dried or frozen.

METRIC/IMPERIAL/AMERICAN
50g/2oz/¼ cup butter or margarine
2 medium cooking apples
1 medium onion, chopped
salt and ground pepper to taste
2 teaspoons dried savory
  or 1 tablespoon chopped fresh savory
4 pork chops
150ml/¼ pint/⅔ cup cider

4 tablespoons/4 tablespoons/⅓ cup
  toasted breadcrumbs
4 tablespoons/4 tablespoons/⅓ cup grated
  cheese
Garnish:
apple rings fried in butter
celery leaves or parsley sprigs

Pork chops
with apples and savory

Butter a shallow ovenproof dish. Peel, core and slice the apples and spread on the base of the dish with the chopped onion and season well. Sprinkle over the savory.

Trim the pork chops, removing the fat, and place on top of the apples. Pour in the cider which should just cover the apples. Mix the breadcrumbs and cheese together and cover each chop. Dot with remaining butter.

Bake in a moderately hot oven (200°C, 400°F, Gas Mark 6) for about 45 minutes or until the chops are tender with a crispy golden crust on top. For the garnish, fry the apple rings in butter and place one on each chop, with a tuft of fresh celery leaves or a sprig of parsley.

French beans
with savory poulette sauce

METRIC/IMPERIAL/AMERICAN
450g/1lb/1lb French beans
salt
50g/2oz/¼ cup butter
1 tablespoon flour
freshly ground pepper

1 teaspoon chopped fresh savory
1 egg yolk
lemon juice to taste
Garnish:
chopped fresh savory

Refresh the beans in cold water until crisp. Top and tail and remove any strings. Cook in just enough boiling salted water to cover. Drain through a colander and keep warm under a dry cloth. Reserve the liquor.

Melt the butter in a small saucepan. Remove from the heat and blend in the flour. Gradually add 300ml/½ pint/1¼ cups of the bean liquor. Bring to the boil, stirring well. Season with freshly ground pepper and mix in the chopped savory. Simmer gently for 5–10 minutes. Beat the egg yolk with a teaspoon of lemon juice and 2 tablespoons/2 tablespoons/3 tablespoons bean liquor. Remove the sauce from heat and blend in the egg mixture. Season to taste with salt, pepper and lemon juice. Keep warm over gentle heat without boiling. Arrange the well-drained beans in a warm serving dish. Pour over the sauce and sprinkle with chopped fresh savory.

Note: Runner beans cut across in 1-cm/½-inch pieces, not finely sliced, young carrots, whole or sliced in rings or wedges, and broad beans are also excellent prepared in this way.

SORREL

The young leaves of both the wild and cultivated sorrel have a very sharp flavour, especially the wild variety, and are used sparingly in raw salads. They have a high water content and, like spinach and lettuce, reduce to a very small volume when cooked. They are usually stewed gently with a little butter, but no water, and because of their acidity, a copper pan should not be used.

Sorrel and bean soup

METRIC/IMPERIAL/AMERICAN
100g/4oz/½ cup haricot beans
1 onion
5–6 cloves
salt
100g/4oz/4oz sorrel leaves
5–6 lettuce leaves
40g/1½oz/3 tablespoons butter

900ml/1½ pints/3¾ cups ham or chicken
   stock
freshly ground pepper
5 tablespoons/5 tablespoons/6 tablespoons
   cream
Garnish:
fried bread croûtons

Soak the beans overnight in cold water. Drain, cover with fresh water, add the onion spiked with cloves and cook until tender. Add salt when they begin to soften. The time taken to cook them will depend on the length of time they have been stored, probably about 2 hours.

Wash the sorrel and lettuce leaves. Chop roughly or tear and put in a pan with the butter. Cover and cook gently until softened. Add the stock and continue cooking for about 15 minutes. Drain the beans when soft and add to the sorrel mixture. Put through a mouli, sieve or liquidize. Return to the pan and heat, stirring steadily. Add a little of the bean liquid if the soup needs thinning and add seasoning. Mix 3–4 tablespoons of the soup with the cream and stir this back into the soup. Serve with croûtons.

Note: This is also very good made with lentils.

METRIC/IMPERIAL/AMERICAN
handful of young sorrel leaves
40g/1½oz/3 tablespoons butter
salt and freshly ground pepper

1 small potato, boiled
1 slice cooked ham
4 eggs

Sorrel omelette
(Serves 2)

Chop or tear the sorrel leaves, discarding the stalks. Put into a small pan with half the butter and season with salt and freshly ground pepper. Cover and cook gently until softened. Drain thoroughly. Dice the cooked potato and ham, discarding any fat. Beat the eggs with a fork and season with salt and pepper. Heat the remaining butter in a large omelette pan and cook the potato and ham lightly for a few minutes.

Pour in the beaten egg and cook quickly, drawing the setting mixture from the edges of the pan and running the liquid egg underneath. When nearly cooked but still liquid in the middle, spoon the sorrel down the centre and fold the omelette over in half. Serve immediately.

SWEET CICELY

This pretty herb is often used as a garnish and it also has a pleasant sweet taste, faintly touched with aniseed which gives fresh fruit salads, compotes and fools a distinctive flavour. It is ideal for calorie counters as it reduces the amount of sugar required in sweet cooked fruit. It is often used in conjunction with lemon balm, and also blends very well with other herbs. Sweet Cicely does not retain its flavour well when dried and is better frozen.

Melon, cucumber and tomato salad

METRIC/IMPERIAL/AMERICAN
8 small tomatoes, skinned
½ cucumber
2 ogen or cantaloupe melons
1 tablespoon chopped sweet Cicely
1 tablespoon chopped fresh chives
1 tablespoon chopped fresh mint
2 tablespoons/2 tablespoons/3 tablespoons
    lemon juice

4 tablespoons/4 tablespoons/⅓ cup salad
    oil
1 teaspoon sugar
salt and freshly ground pepper
Garnish:
sweet Cicely leaves

Cut the tomatoes into quarters, discard the seeds and collect any juice. Cut the tomato flesh into neat pieces.

Wipe and dice the unpeeled cucumber. Halve the melons, discard the seeds and scoop out the flesh in balls with a vegetable scoop. Reserve the shells. Mix with the tomatoes, cucumber and chopped fresh herbs.

Whisk together the lemon juice, oil and juice from the tomatoes. Season to taste with sugar, salt and pepper. Pour over the vegetables and mix well.

Fill the melon shells, cover with cling film and refrigerate until required. Serve well chilled, garnished with sweet Cicely leaves, as a first course.
Note: Tarragon vinegar can be used instead of lemon juice and orange sections instead of the tomatoes.

Rhubarb and sweet Cicely fool

METRIC/IMPERIAL/AMERICAN
450g/1lb/1lb rhubarb
juice and grated rind of 1 orange
1 tablespoon chopped sweet Cicely
sugar to taste
300ml/½ pint/1¼ cups whipped cream
    or 150ml/¼ pint/⅔ cup each of cream
    and custard

Garnish:
sweet Cicely sprigs

Wipe the rhubarb, chop into 2·5-cm/1-inch pieces, discarding the leaves and white ends of the stalks. Put the orange juice into a flameproof casserole with the rhubarb, sweet Cicely and grated orange rind. Cover and bake in a moderate oven (180°C, 350°F, Gas Mark 4) for 20 minutes until soft. Remove from the oven and cook without lid over moderate heat into a thick purée, stirring frequently. Sweeten to taste and cool.

When cold, fold in the whipped cream and custard if used. Spoon into goblets and chill until required. Decorate with little sprigs of sweet Cicely. Serve with crisp sweet biscuits or sponge fingers.

TARRAGON

There are two varieties of tarragon, French and Russian, and it is the former that has the delightful aromatic leaves. They freeze well but lose flavour when dried. The flavour is particularly good with chicken, fish, vegetables and salads and is an integral part of various sauces and savoury butters. Fresh sprigs are used to flavour wine vinegar and salad dressings.

METRIC/IMPERIAL/AMERICAN
40g/1½oz/3 tablespoons butter
40g/1½oz/6 tablespoons flour
900ml/1½ pints/3¾ cups chicken stock
225g/8oz/8oz button mushrooms

2 teaspoons chopped fresh tarragon
300ml/½ pint/1¼ cups single cream
Garnish:
fresh tarragon leaves

Melt the butter, remove from the heat and blend in the flour then the chicken stock. Return to the heat and simmer gently for 10–15 minutes, stirring. Meanwhile, wash the mushrooms and put through a mouli, sieve or liquidizer.

Add the mushroom pulp to the soup with the chopped tarragon and stir in the cream. Simmer for 4–5 minutes, then pour into a cold bowl and whisk occasionally while cooling. When cold, refrigerate until required. Whisk again before serving, pour into soup cups and garnish with a few leaves of fresh tarragon.

Pot-roasted chicken
with tarragon

METRIC/IMPERIAL/AMERICAN
1 (1·25-kg/2½-lb/2½-lb) chicken, dressed
40g/1½oz/3 tablespoons butter, creamed
1 tablespoon chopped fresh tarragon
1 small clove garlic, pressed
salt and freshly ground pepper
olive oil for basting
6–8 button onions, peeled
1 stick celery, chopped
100ml/4floz/½ cup white wine

3–4 tablespoons/3–4 tablespoons/4–5
   tablespoons soured cream
Giblet stock:
chicken giblets
bouquet garni
salt
6 black peppercorns
Garnish:
fresh tarragon leaves

Truss the chicken neatly. Cream together the butter, chopped tarragon and pressed garlic and season with salt and freshly ground pepper. Put this inside the chicken and brush all over chicken liberally with olive oil. Heat a tablespoon of oil in a deep flameproof casserole and brown the chicken all over on a brisk heat. Add the onions and celery. Season with salt and freshly ground pepper. Add the white wine, simmer for a minute, lower the heat, cover and cook very gently for 45 minutes, turning the chicken from time to time.

Meanwhile, clean the giblets, cover with cold water, add a bouquet garni (see page 126), salt and peppercorns. Cover and simmer gently until required.

Test the leg of the chicken. If the juice runs amber coloured, the chicken is cooked, if it runs red, continue cooking gently until done. Add a little giblet stock to the casserole if the liquid has evaporated.

When the chicken is cooked, remove from the casserole, tipping it so the juices inside run out into the casserole. Add a cupful of giblet stock, boil briskly to reduce. Mix together the soured cream with 3–4 tablespoons of chicken gravy, pour this into the casserole and heat through. Adjust the seasoning.

Replace the chicken in the casserole and garnish with fresh tarragon leaves or serve the chicken on a platter and hand the sauce separately.

METRIC/IMPERIAL/AMERICAN
2 large chicory heads
1 orange
175ml/6floz/¾ cup soured cream
1 hard-boiled egg yolk, sieved
1 teaspoon continental mustard
1–2 teaspoons castor sugar

2 teaspoons tarragon vinegar
salt and black pepper to taste
2 teaspoons chopped fresh tarragon leaves
Garnish:
tarragon sprig

Chicory and orange salad
with tarragon cream dressing
Illustrated on page 105

Wash the chicory heads, discard any discoloured leaves and pull off several for garnish. Slice the heads and break into rings. Peel the orange, remove the pith, cut down between the membranes with a sharp knife and lift out the sections. In a bowl, mix together the soured cream, sieved egg yolk, mustard, sugar, tarragon vinegar and salt and pepper to taste. Stir in the chopped tarragon leaves. Mix in the sliced chicory. Line a salad dish with the chicory leaves. Put the dressed salad in the centre and garnish with the orange sections and a sprig of tarragon.

THYME

The lemon-flavoured thyme is best for cooking. It is good on its own and blends well with other herbs. A sprig of thyme is essential in a bouquet garni. The flavour is at its best in summer when it should be picked for drying and freezing. The stalk can be chopped with the leaves when young, but the leaves only should be used when more mature.

Lambs' kidneys in sherry sauce

METRIC/IMPERIAL/AMERICAN
450g/1lb/1lb lambs' kidneys
50g/2oz/¼ cup butter
1 large onion, sliced
100g/4oz/4oz mushrooms
4 large tomatoes, skinned
1 teaspoon chopped lemon thyme
  or ½ teaspoon dried lemon thyme
3 tablespoons/3 tablespoons/ ¼ cup brown
  sherry or sweet Vermouth
salt and freshly ground pepper
1 teaspoon sugar
stock or bouillon

Halve the kidneys, skin and remove the fatty core with scissors. Heat the butter in a sauté pan, fry the kidneys briskly and remove from the pan. Be careful not to overcook or they will become hard. Fry the sliced onion gently until transparent. Add the mushroom caps and chopped stalks and sauté until softened. Chop and add the skinned tomatoes and lemon thyme. Cover and cook gently over moderate heat for about 5 minutes, shaking the pan from time to time. Add the sherry and kidneys and season with salt, pepper and sugar. Add a little stock if required and simmer gently for about 10 minutes or until cooked.

Serve with boiled new potatoes, rice or pasta.

Note: This dish can also be made with 350g/12oz/12oz sliced lambs' or calf liver or 4 portions of well hung rump steak.

Cider-baked onions

Illustrated on page 96

METRIC/IMPERIAL/AMERICAN
4 medium onions
40g/1½oz/3 tablespoons butter or 2
  tablespoons/2 tablespoons/3 tablespoons olive oil
2 teaspoons chopped fresh lemon thyme
  or 1 teaspoon dried lemon thyme
2 teaspoons chopped fresh sage or
  1 teaspoon dried sage
salt and freshly ground pepper
3–4 tablespoons/2–3fl oz/¼–⅓ cup cider
Garnish:
chopped fresh thyme or other fresh
  herbs

Peel the onions, cut off the roots and slice off the top. Cut the onions across in half. Heat the butter or oil in a shallow flameproof casserole or gratin dish. Place the onions, centre downwards, in the casserole and fry until golden. Remove from the heat, turn the onions upwards, sprinkle with herbs and season well with salt and freshly ground pepper. Pour in sufficient cider to cover the base of the casserole, cover with a lid or foil.

Bake in a moderately hot oven (190°C, 375°F, Gas Mark 5) for 45 minutes to 1 hour, according to thickness, until tender. Just before serving, spoon the cooking liquid over the onions and sprinkle with fresh herbs.

HERB STUFFINGS, DUMPLINGS, SAUCES AND BUTTERS

Pineapple and mint stuffing

(For roasts)

METRIC/IMPERIAL/AMERICAN
40g/1½oz/3 tablespoons butter or
  margarine
1 medium onion, finely chopped
100g/4oz/1 cup celery, finely chopped
100g/4oz/1 cup carrots, finely chopped
2 tablespoons/2 tablespoons/3 tablespoons
  chopped fresh mint

50g/2oz/¼ cup rice, cooked
4 rings pineapple, fresh or canned
1 teaspoon paprika
salt and freshly ground pepper
lemon juice to taste

Heat the butter and fry the onion and celery gently until softened. Add the carrot, mint and rice and cook for 2–3 minutes, stirring well. Chop and add the pineapple with the paprika. Season well with salt, pepper and lemon juice.

This is an excellent stuffing for lamb guard of honour or crown of lamb (see page 115).
Variations: For roast pork, duck and goose, substitute sage, savory or parsley for the mint.

For chicken and guinea fowl, substitute tarragon or rosemary for the mint and add 2 tablespoons/2 tablespoons/3 tablespoons sultanas. For turkey, increase the quantity according to the size of the bird.

Herb dumplings
and stuffing balls

METRIC/IMPERIAL/AMERICAN
175g/6oz/1½ cups self-raising flour
salt and freshly ground pepper
1 tablespoon chopped fresh parsley

1 teaspoon chopped chives
1–2 teaspoons chopped herbs*
75g/3oz/⅔ cup shredded suet

* For lamb and veal, flavour with mint or rosemary. For pork and hare, flavour with savory or sage.
Mix together the flour, seasoning, herbs and suet. Stir in sufficient cold water to make a stiff dough. Divide into 8 equal portions and roll into small balls.
Dumplings for stews and casseroles: Put the dumplings on top of the meat and vegetables in a stewpan or casserole, cover and cook for 30 minutes until well-risen and fluffy.
Crunchy dumplings for roasts: Put in the hot fat round the roasting joint and bake for 30 minutes until crisp and golden.
Stuffing balls for hare: Coat in egg and breadcrumbs and fry in deep fat; garnish jugged hare.

METRIC/IMPERIAL/AMERICAN
½ cupful spinach leaves
1 cupful parsley sprigs
4 tarragon sprigs
4 chervil sprigs

300ml/½ pint/1¼ cups mayonnaise
2 tablespoons/2 tablespoons/3 tablespoons
  cream
salt and freshly ground pepper

Green mayonnaise

(For salmon and cold fish)

Wash and cook the spinach, parsley, tarragon and chervil in just enough boiling salted water to cover until tender. Drain thoroughly pressing it with a saucer until dry. Put the pulp through a mouli or sieve and stir the purée into the mayonnaise. Stir in the cream and season to taste with salt and freshly ground pepper. Chill before serving.

Horseradish sauce

(For beef, smoked fish and shellfish salads)

METRIC/IMPERIAL/AMERICAN
150ml/¼ pint/⅔ cup soured cream
dash mild mustard
1–2 tablespoons/1–2 tablespoons/1–3
   tablespoons grated horseradish

sugar
salt and pepper to taste

Mix the soured cream with the mustard. Stir in the grated horseradish. (The amount needed will vary according to the strength of the horseradish.) Add sugar to taste and season with salt and freshly ground pepper.
Note: If soured cream is not available, add 2 teaspoons lemon juice to 150ml/¼ pint/⅔ cup double cream.

Bouquet garni

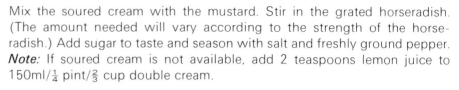

A bay leaf is an indispensable ingredient of the little bunch of fresh or dried herbs called a 'bouquet garni', which is used in so many stocks, soups and casserole dishes. The other essential fresh herbs are 2 or 3 sprigs of leaves and stalks of parsley, one of thyme and sometimes celery.

The faggot is tied together with a piece of string long enough to tie round the handle of the pan so the bouquet can be withdrawn when required. Elizabeth David says she finds the preparing of herb bouquets one of the 'minor pleasures' of cooking and even more so if they are your own home-grown herbs.

If you are using dried herbs it is better to tie them in a little muslin bag and add a crushed clove of garlic and a few peppercorns; sometimes juniper berries or a piece of orange or lemon rind are also added.

Herb butters

Illustrated on pages 108–9

Garlic butter
Finely chop or press 3–4 garlic cloves and beat into 100g/4oz/½ cup softened salted butter.

Maître d'Hôtel butter (Parsley)
Add 4 tablespoons/4 tablespoons/⅓ cup finely chopped fresh parsley to 100g/4oz/½ cup softened salted butter. Sharpen to taste with lemon juice.

Montpelier butter (Green butter for grilled and cold fish)
Blanch in boiling salted water, 4 tablespoons/4 tablespoons/⅓ cup each of parsley, chervil, cress, chives and spinach, for 5 minutes. Drain, press dry in soft kitchen paper. Sieve or blend in a liquidizer and work in 100g/4oz/½ cup softened butter. Pound 2 anchovy fillets in a mortar and add. Sharpen with 1 teaspoon grated lemon rind and season well.
Note: Use finely chopped fresh green herbs to flavour herb butters, beaten into softened salted butter and sharpened with a little lemon juice. The proportion varies according to the strength of the herbs. To 100g/4oz/½ cup butter, you can add up to 4 tablespoons/4 tablespoons/⅓ cup parsley, mint, tarragon, chervil, chives or salad burnet, individually or a mixture. Use about 3 tablespoons/3 tablespoons/¼ cup or less of sage, savory, thyme, marjoram or basil.

Index